BUSINESS CAT
MONEY POWER TREATS

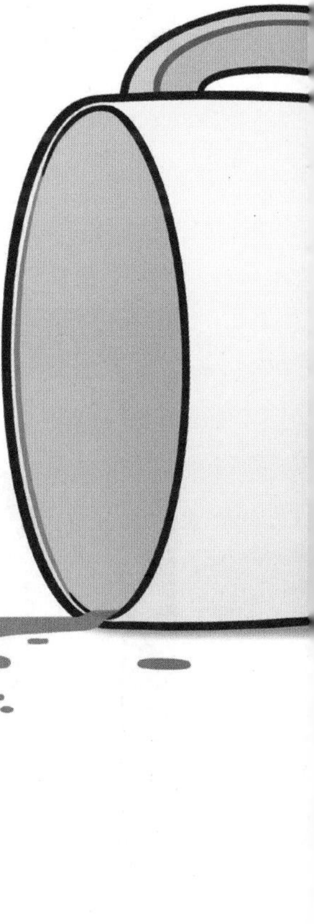

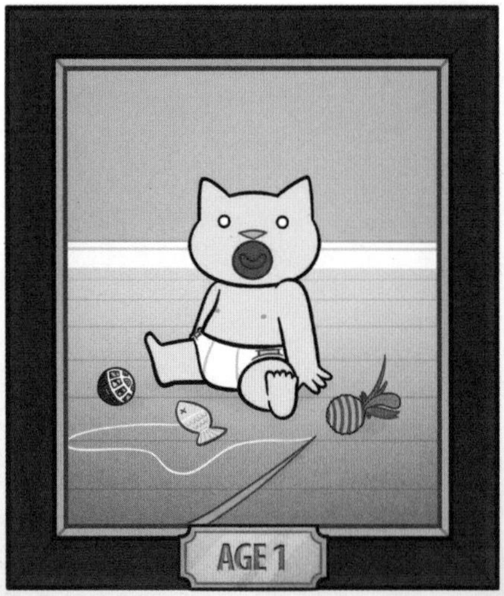
AGE 1

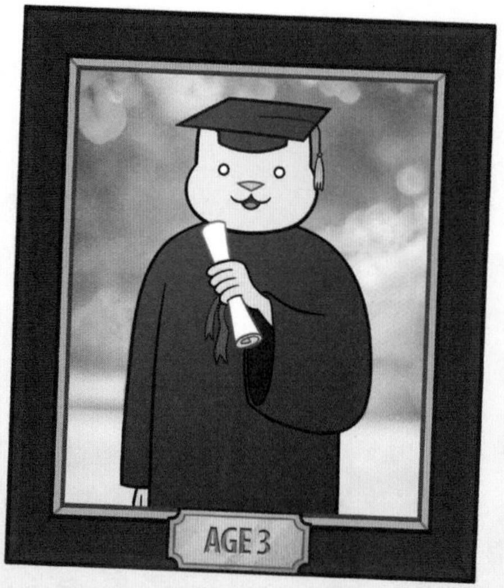
AGE 3

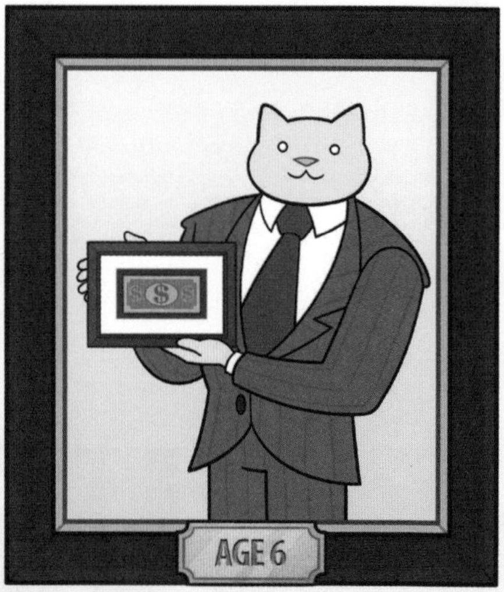
AGE 6

for Rachael

without you, none of this is possible

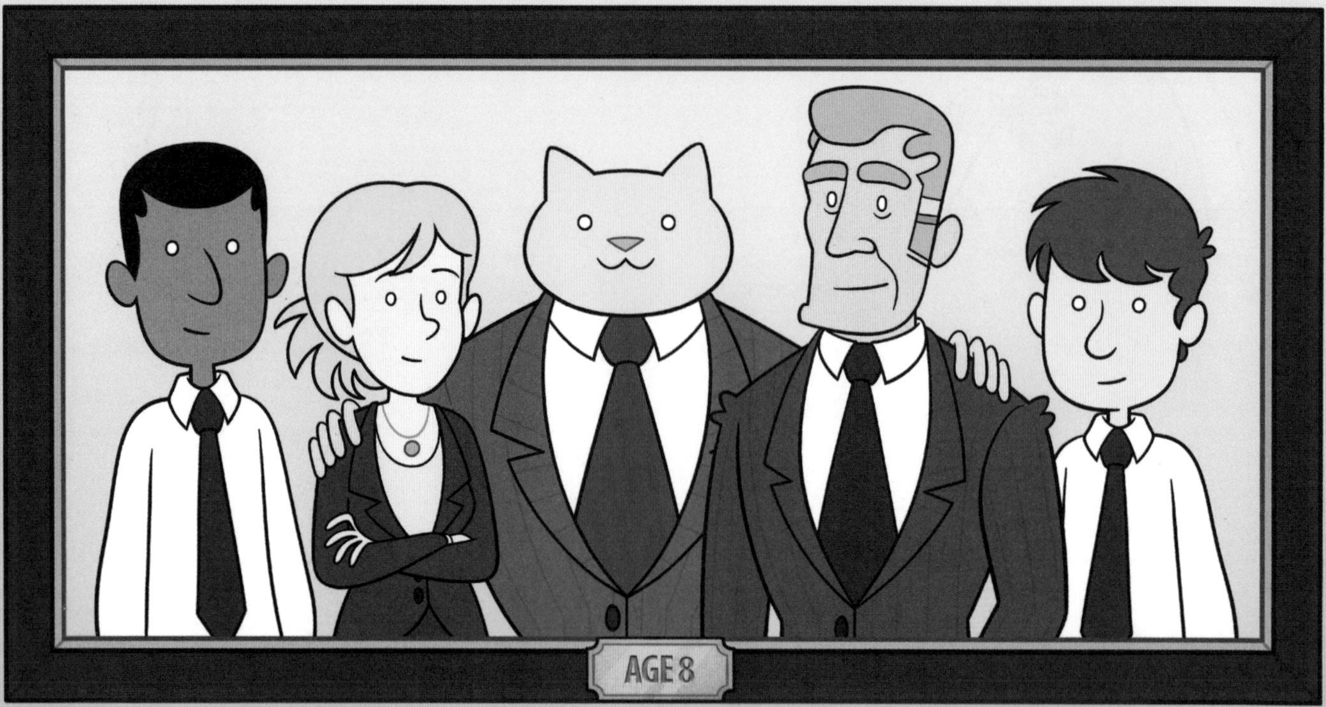
AGE 8

BUSINESS CAT
MONEY POWER TREATS

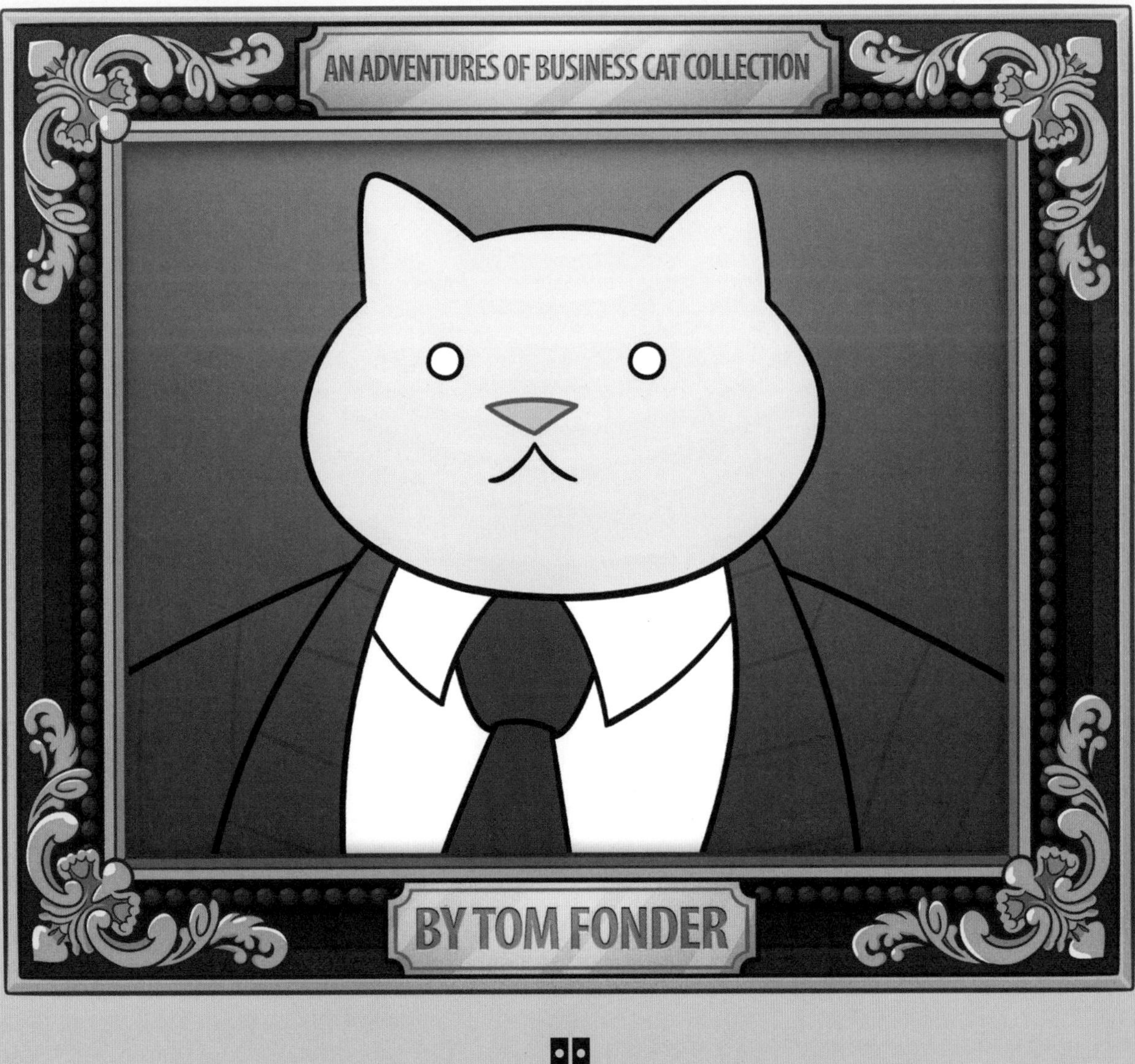
AN ADVENTURES OF BUSINESS CAT COLLECTION
BY TOM FONDER

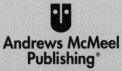

Andrews McMeel
Publishing®
a division of Andrews McMeel Universal

CLICK.

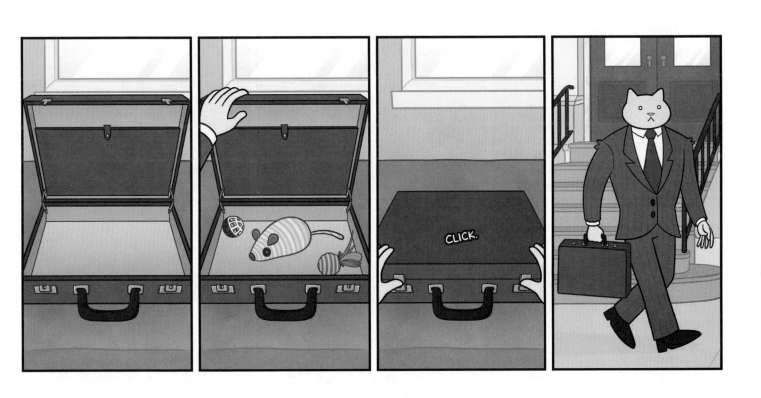

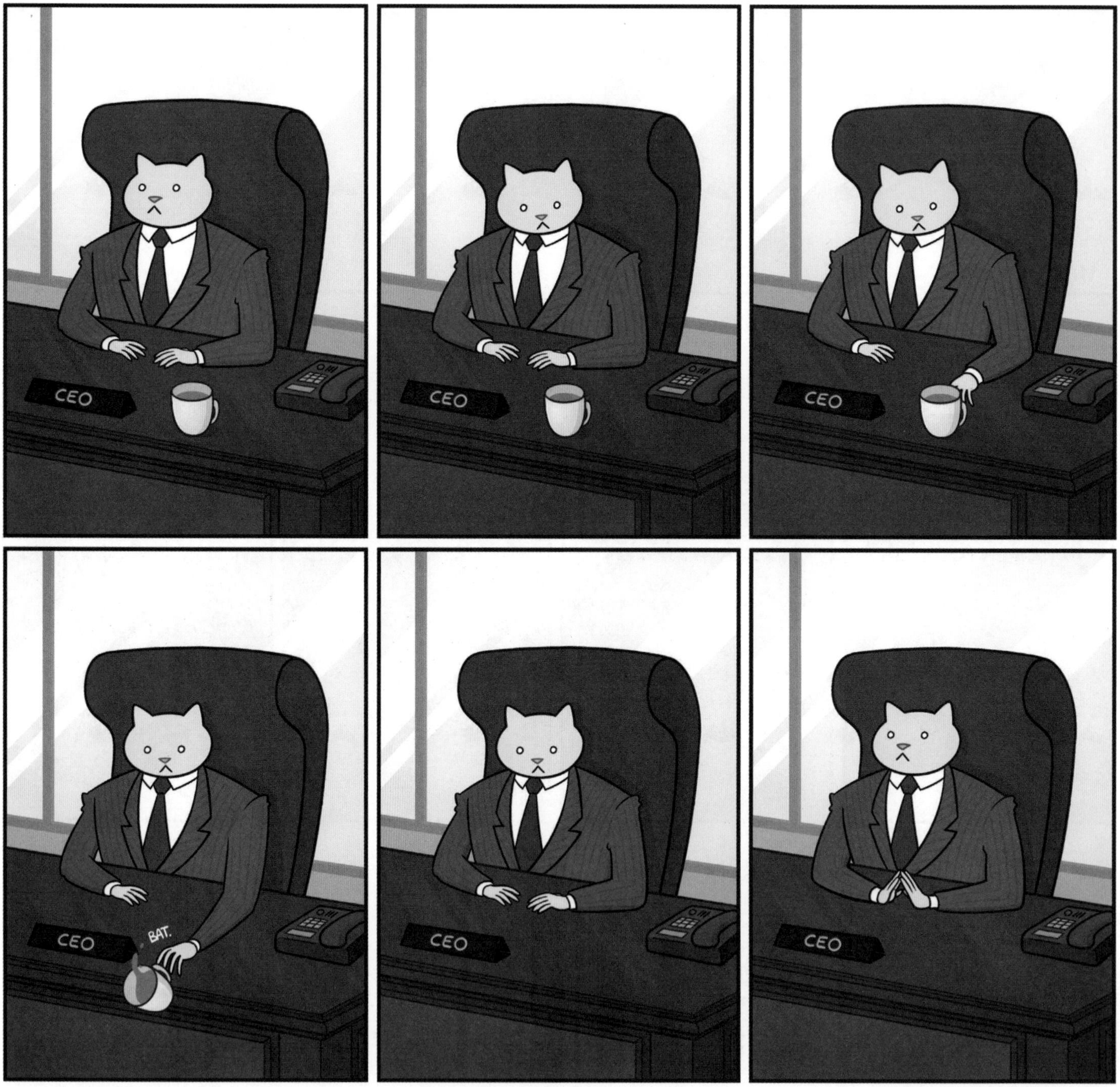
CEO
CEO
CEO
CEO
BAT.
CEO
CEO

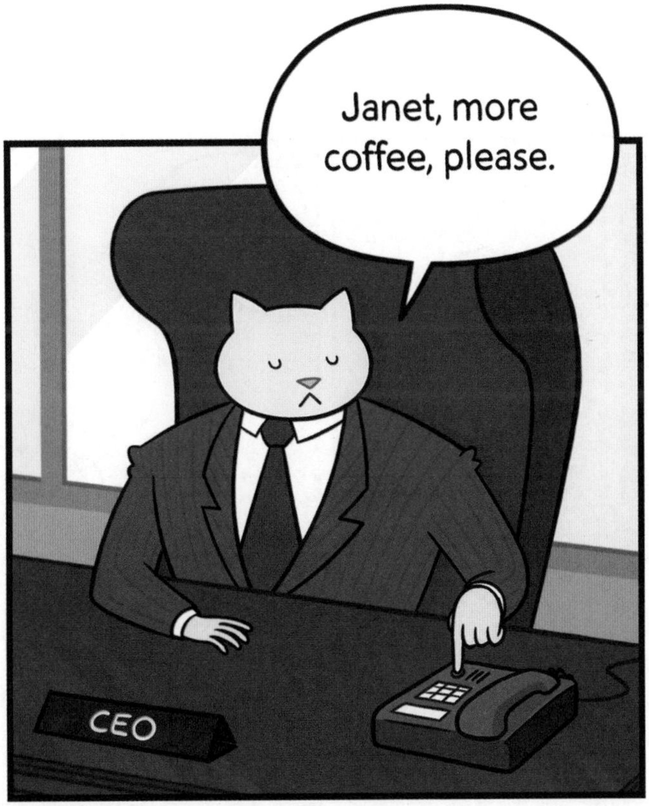
Janet, more coffee, please.
CEO

Hey.
You've earned it.

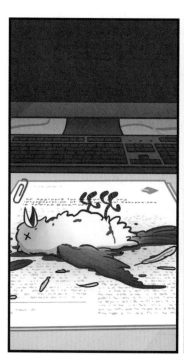

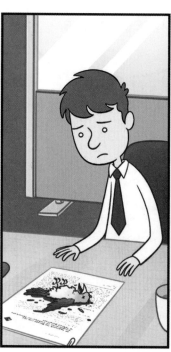

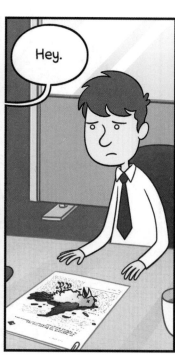

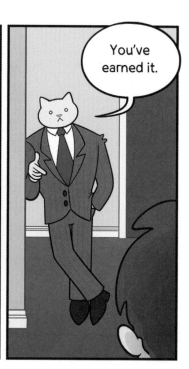

HANG IN THERE, BABY!
HANG IN THERE, BABY!

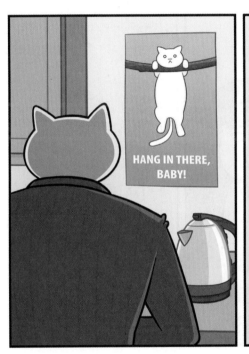

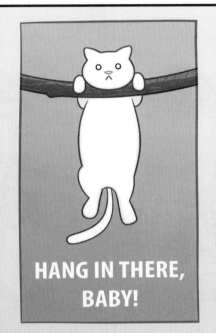

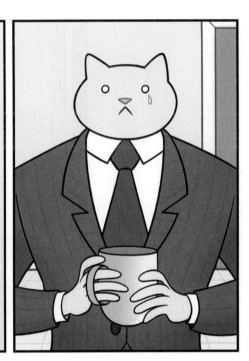

We need to land this account with Tokyo Motor. It's imperative we make a good impression.
Got it.
Time to dial up the charm.
Gentlemen.

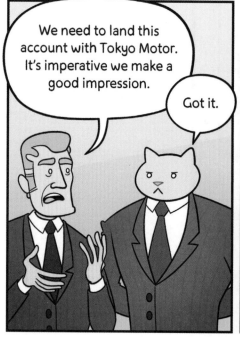

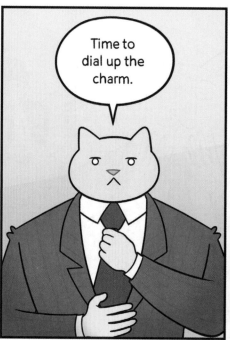

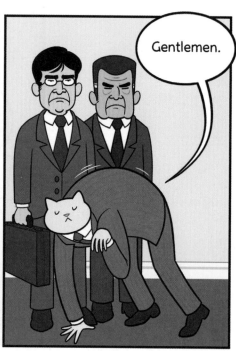

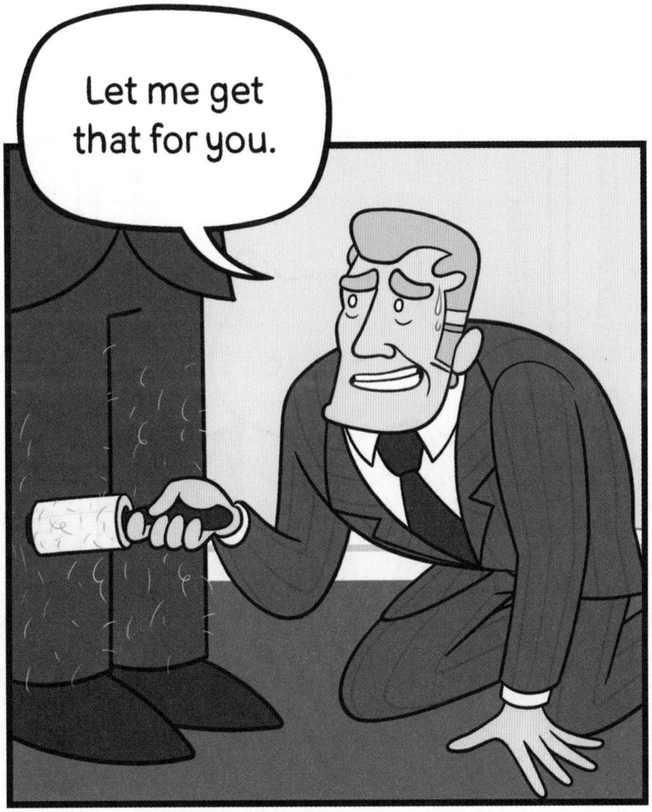
Let me get that for you.

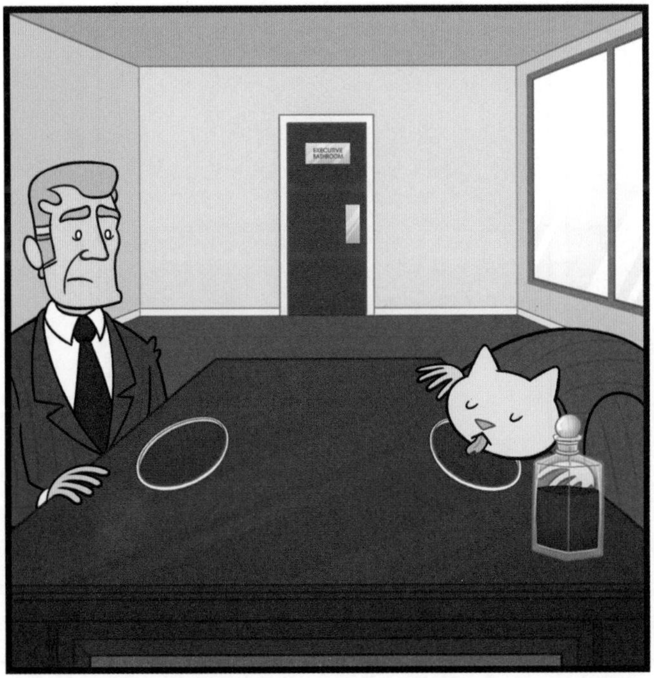
EXECUTIVE BATHROOM

Here are those reports you asked for.
Thank you, Janet. That will be all.
CEO
CEO

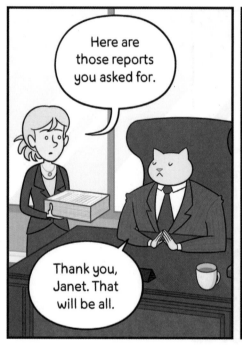

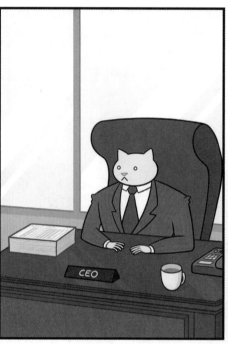

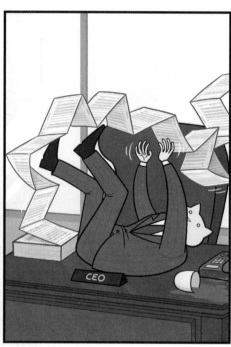

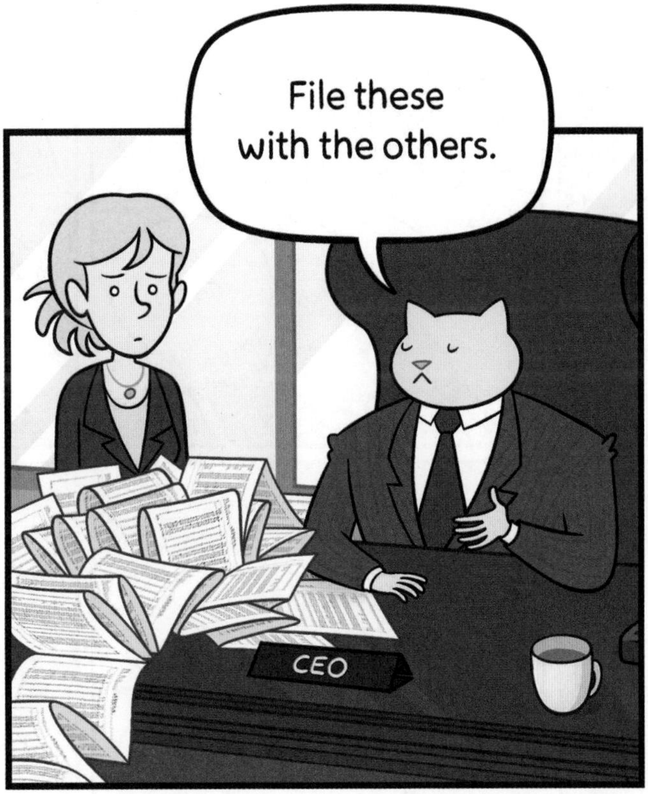
File these with the others.
CEO

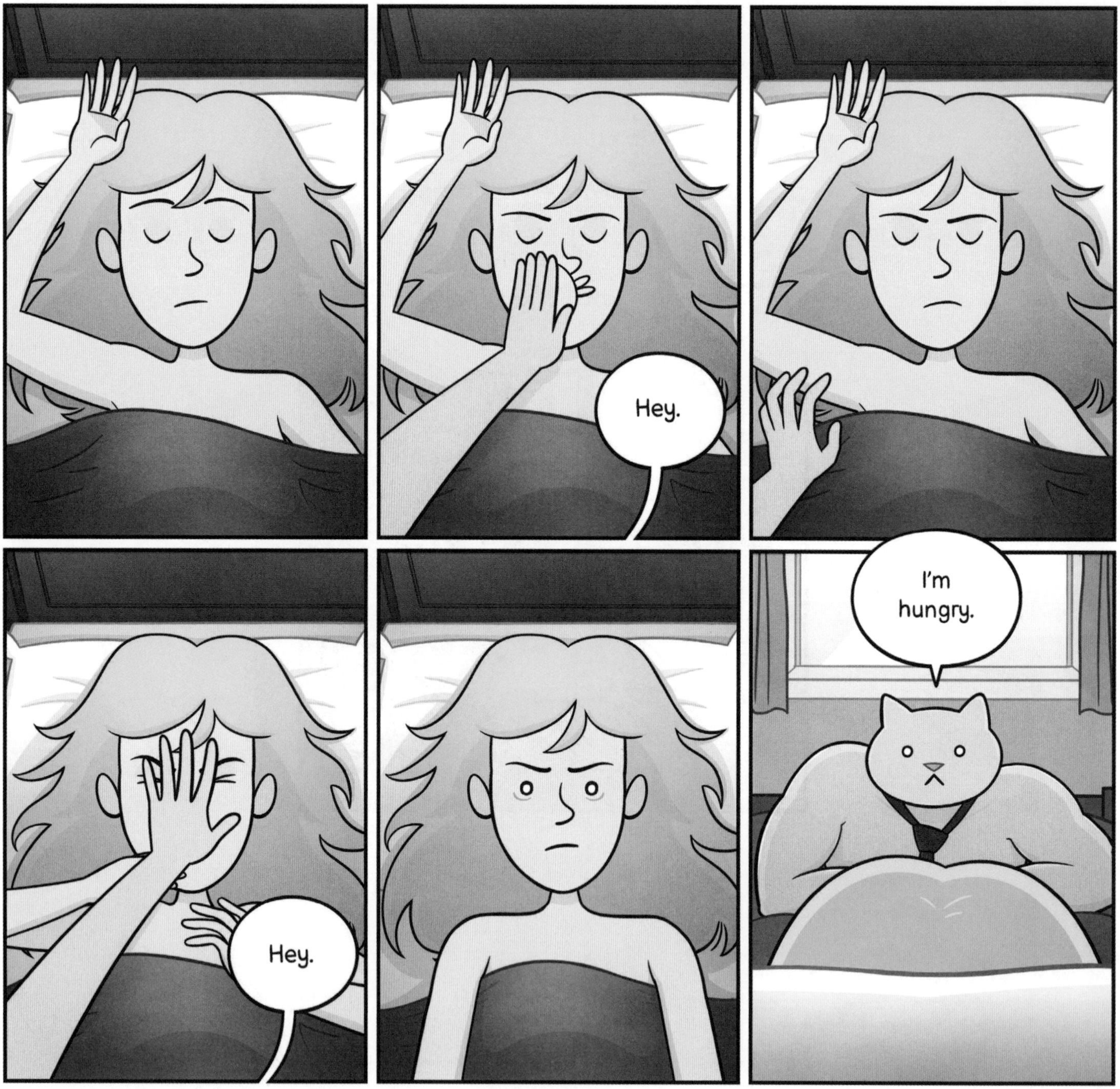
Hey.
Hey.
I'm hungry.

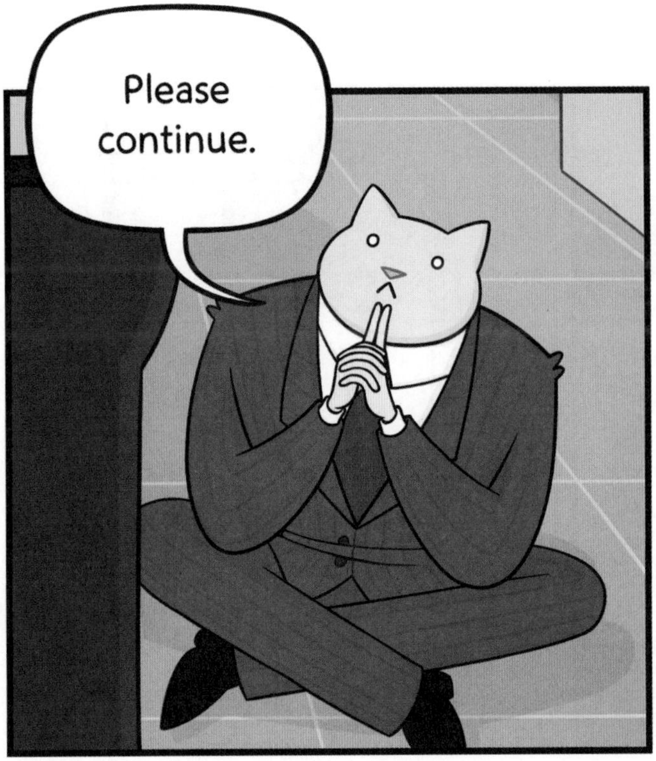
Please continue.

EXECUTIVE
BATHROOM

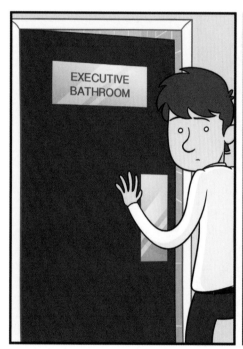

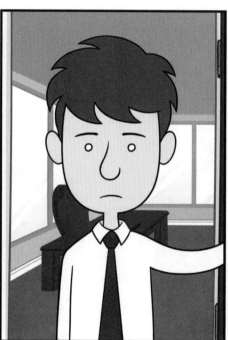

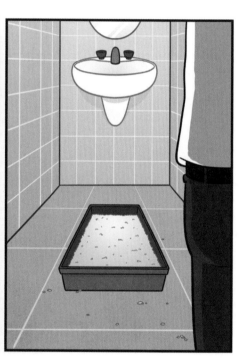

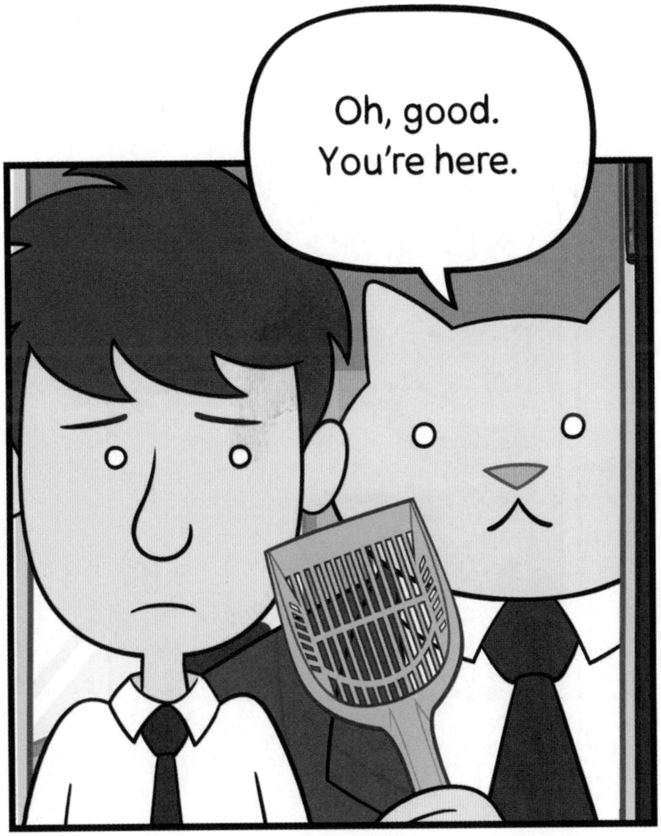
Oh, good.
You're here.

Hey, the new photocopier arrived.
Excellent.
TRASH
OFFICE STUFF PTY LTD

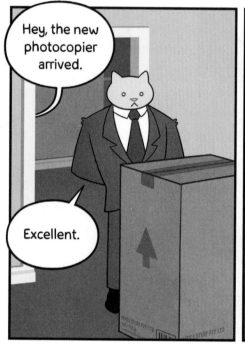

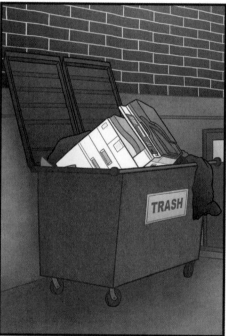

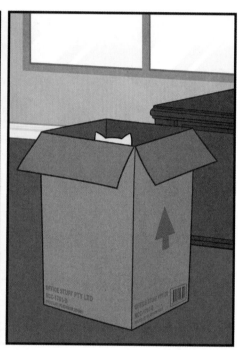

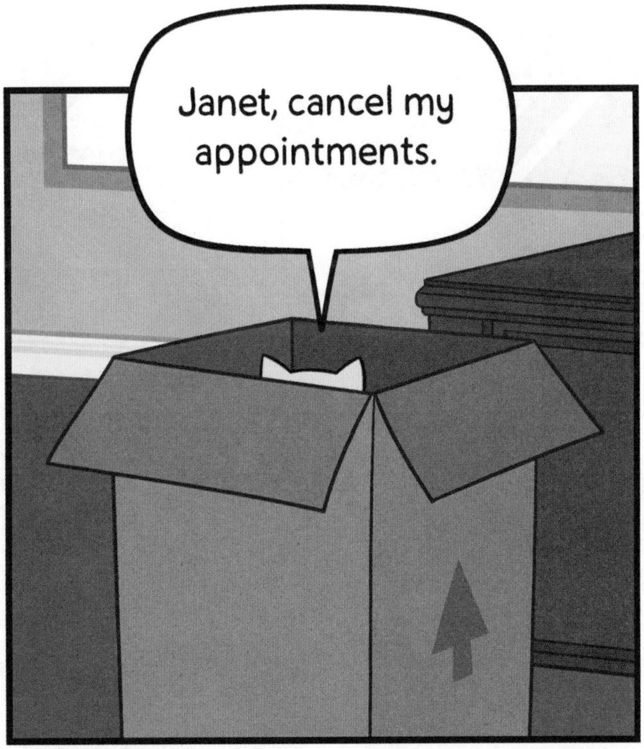
Janet, cancel my appointments.

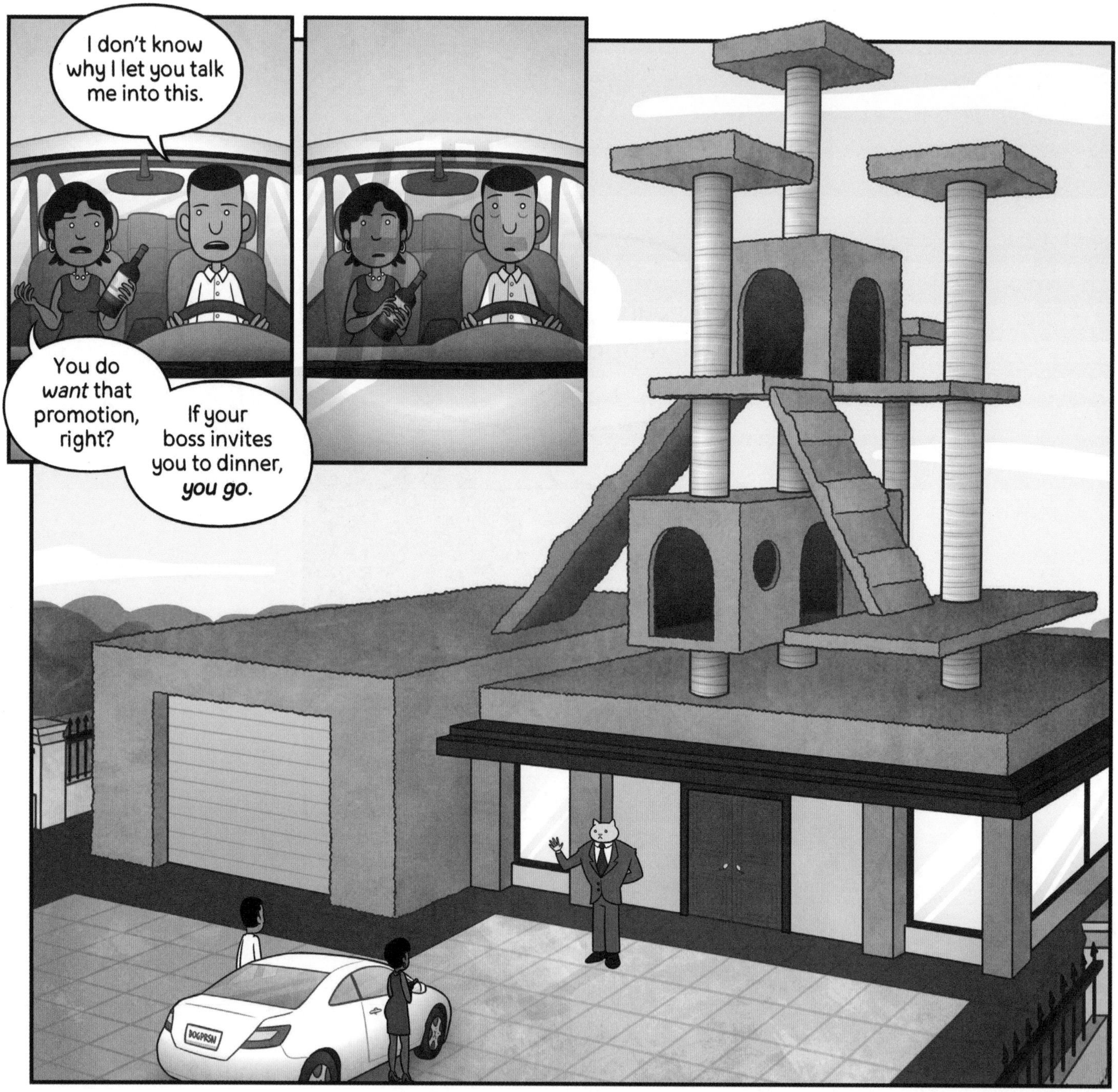
I don't know why I let you talk me into this.
You do *want* that promotion, right?
If your boss invites you to dinner, ***you go***.
DOGPRSN

Sorry about the mess. Looks like Kevin's been at his toys.
Oh. You... have a cat?
Yeah, here he is now. Say hi to Rob and Kayla, Kevin!

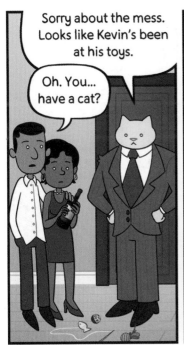

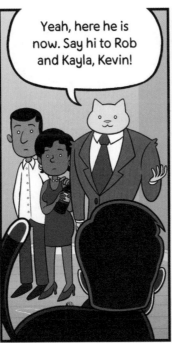

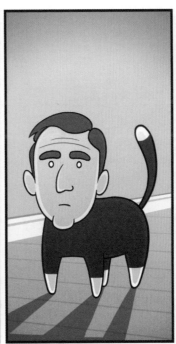

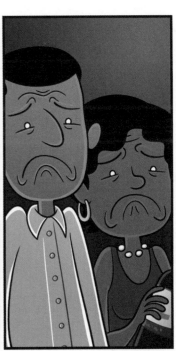

I caught them myself.

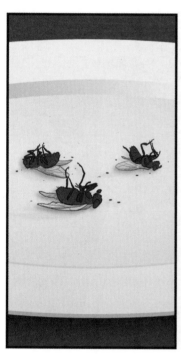

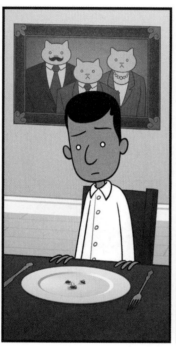

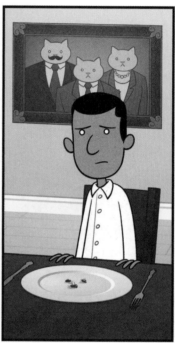

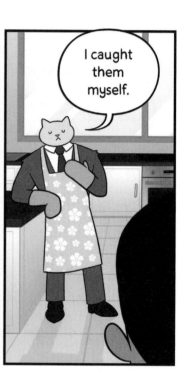

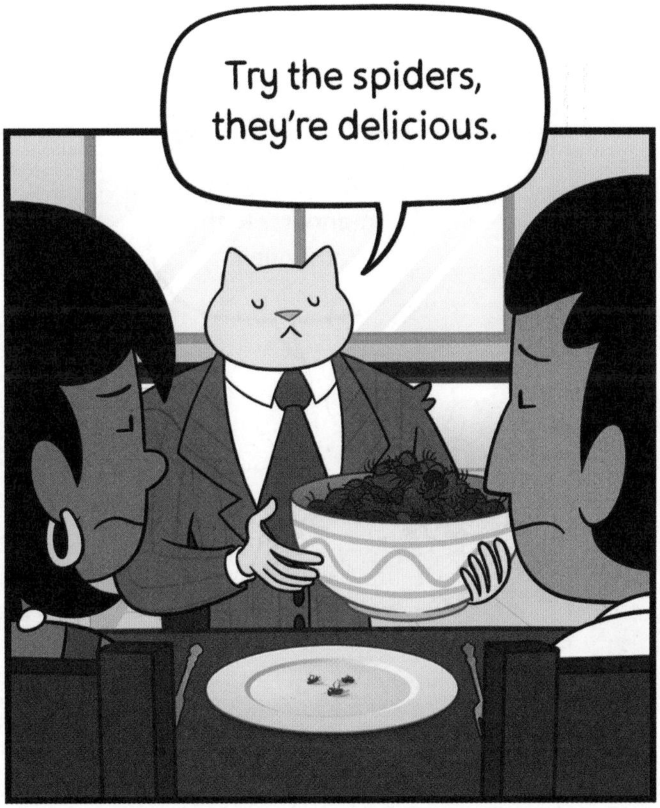
Try the spiders, they're delicious.

Do you think I could use your bathroom?
Where are my manners? Right this way.
Cover up when you're finished.

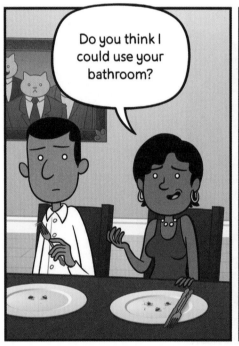

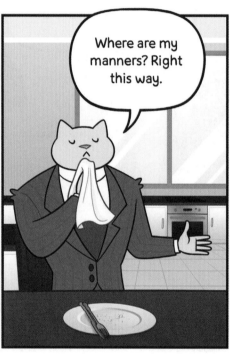

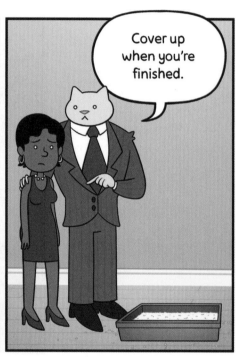

If you'd care to join me in the rumpus room, I've prepared some evening entertainment.

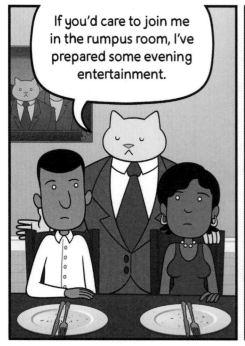

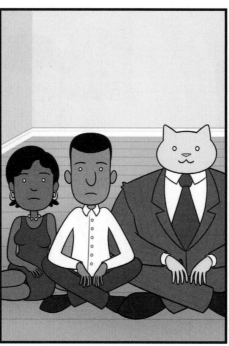

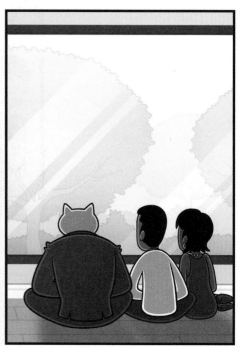

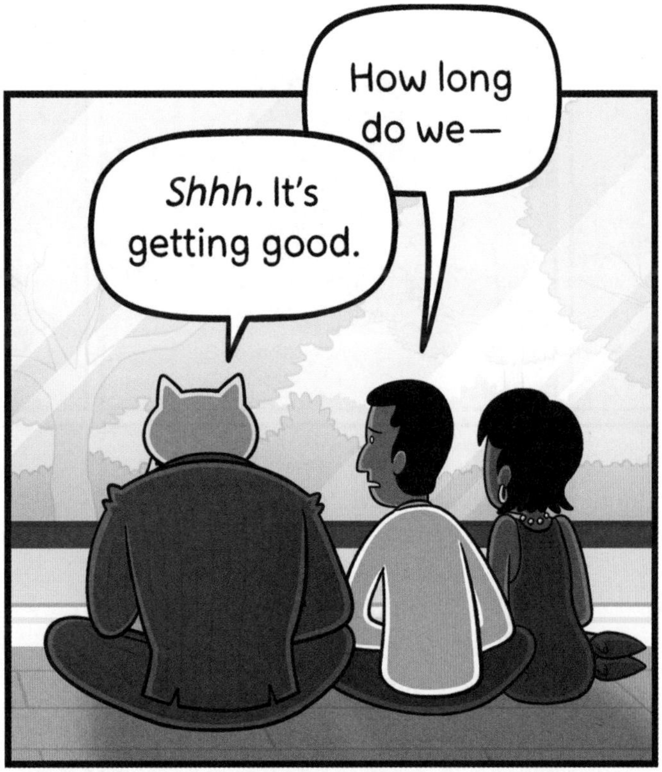
How long do we—
Shhh. It's getting good.

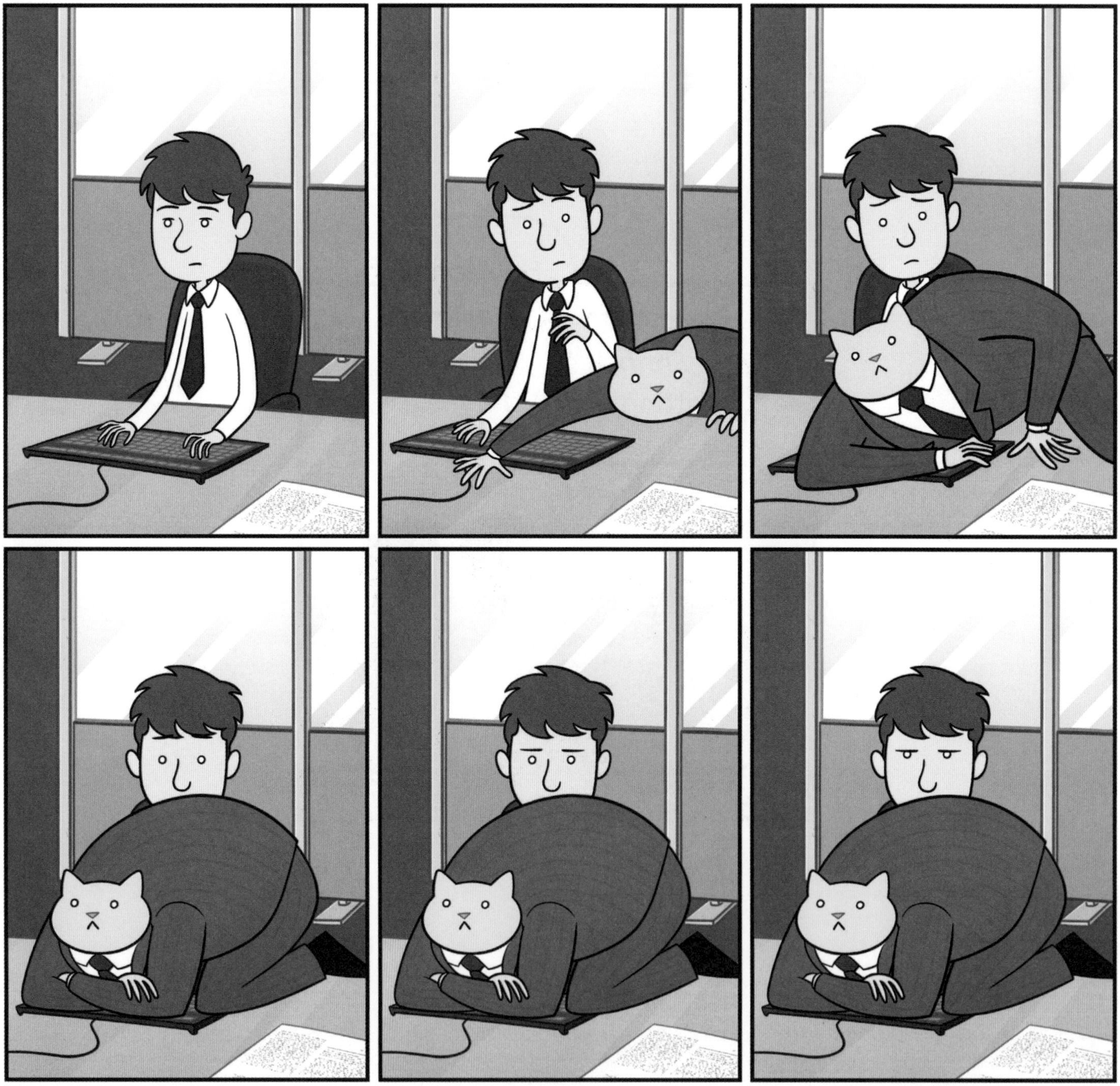

Jesus. What happened?
There was an altercation.

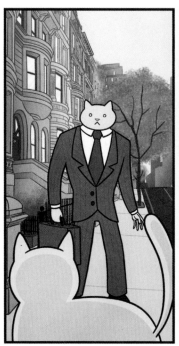

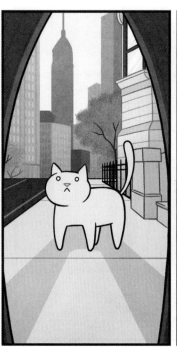

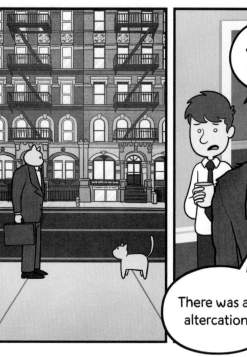

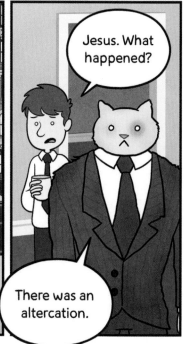

Janet, hold my calls. I have a doctor's appointment.
Mr. Cat? Consult room three.
BODY SHAME
CHANEL
I think that's me.

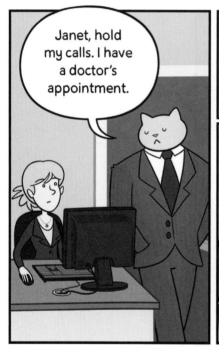

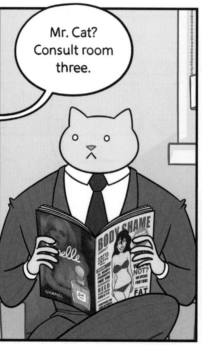

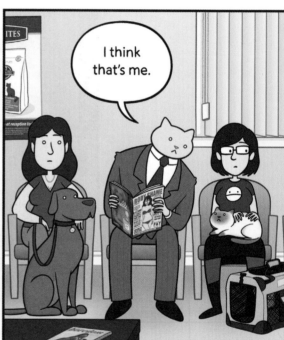

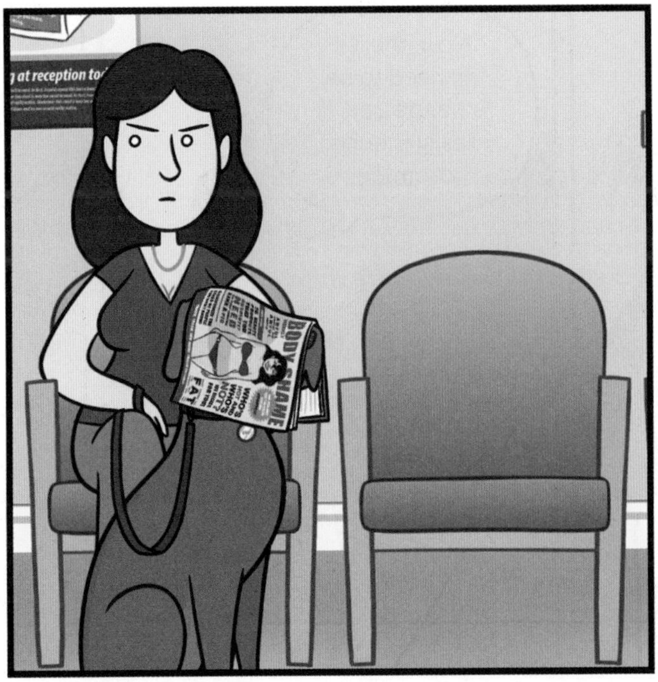
at reception to
BODY SHAME
NEED
WHO'S HOT AND WHO'S NOT?
FAT

Well, it's just as I suspected. You have fleas.
FELINE ANATOMY
Oh, God.
Now, there's no need to be embarrassed. It really is quite common.
FELINE ANATOMY
But I *do* need to ask that you notify any previous partners.
FELINE ANATOMY

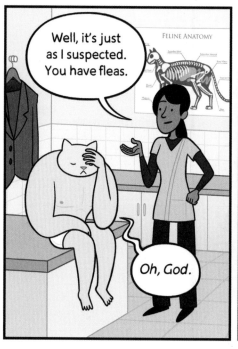

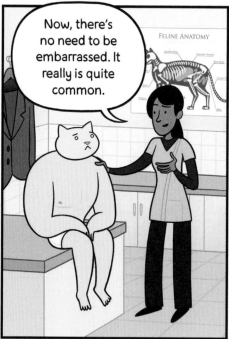

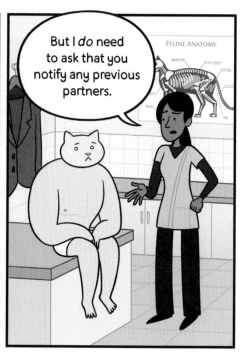

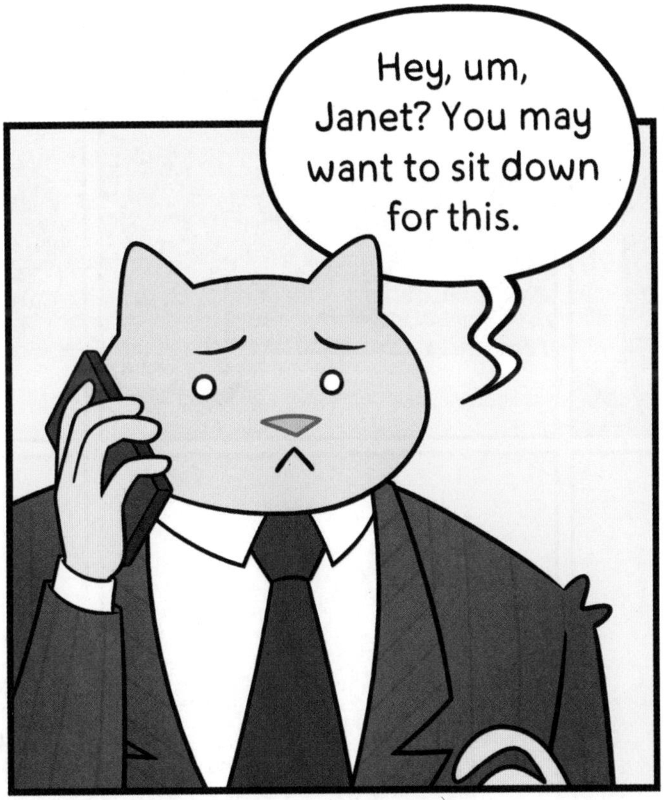
Hey, um, Janet? You may want to sit down for this.

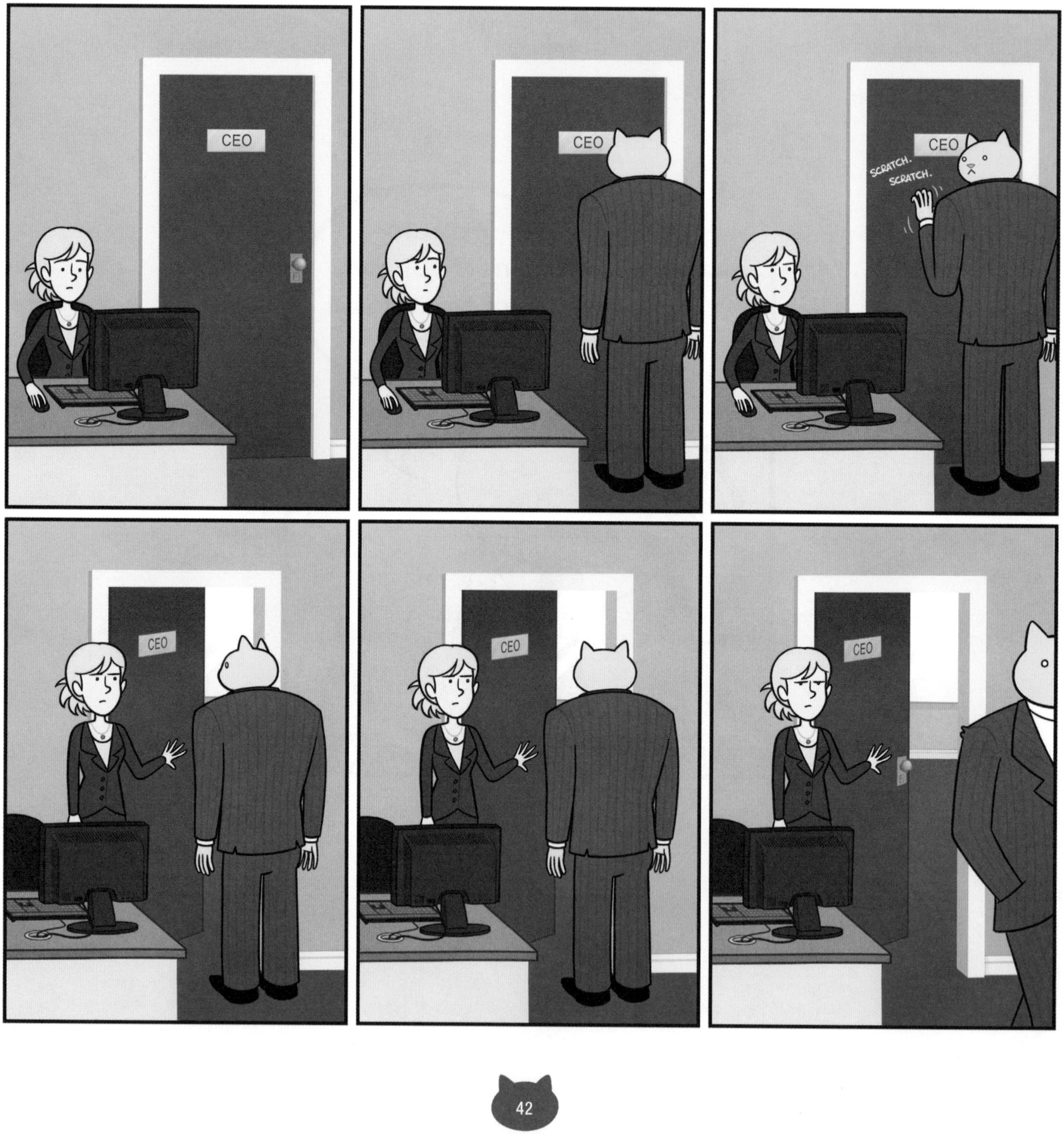
CEO
SCRATCH.
SCRATCH.

...and here's *your* Secret Santa, Rob.
Oh. Wow. Jesus.
I wonder who this could be from...

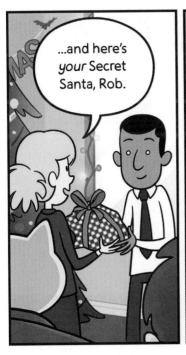

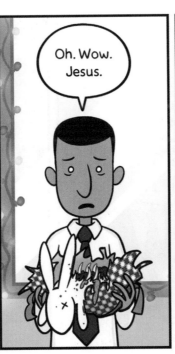

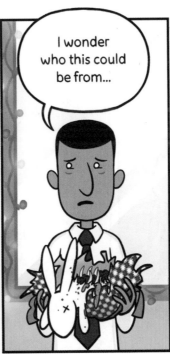

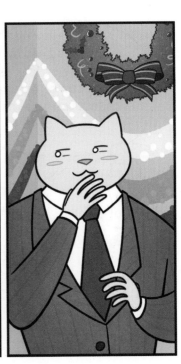

Ted. I need you to do a write-up for the presentation on Monday. I'll shoot you an e-mail with the deets.
tps://mail.google.com/mail/u/0/#inbox/pr1s0nr24601
Deets
Inbox
from:
Business Cat <businesscat@petmail.com>
to me
Click here to Reply or Forward

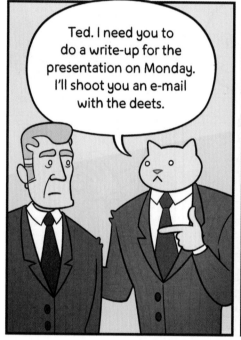

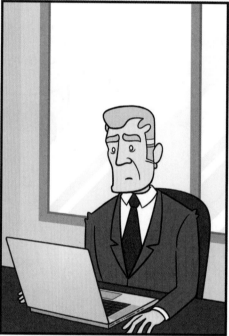

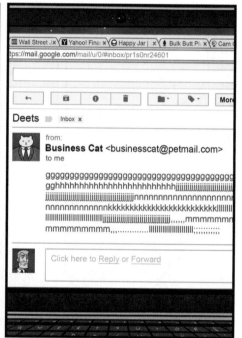

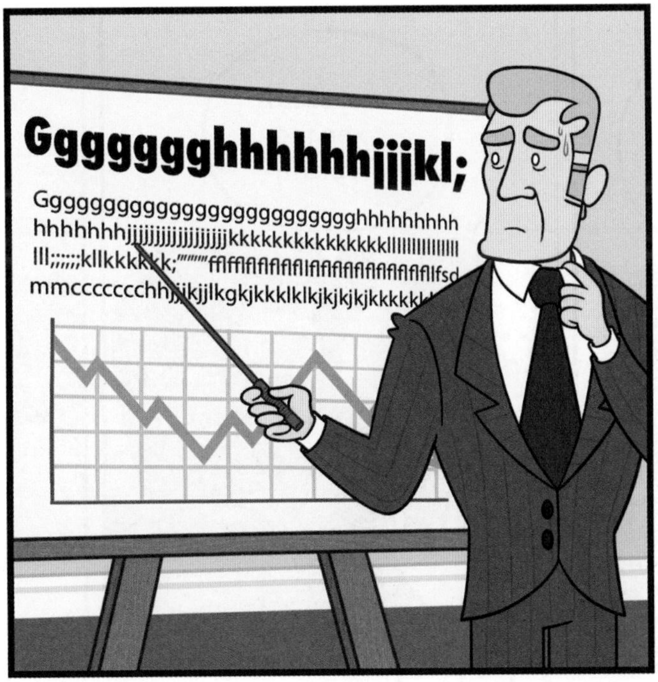
Ggggggghhhhhhjjjkl;

Janet, get someone from IT up here. There's something wrong with my computer.
CEO
What seems to be the problem?
CEO
The birds on the YouTube. I cannot get them.
CEO

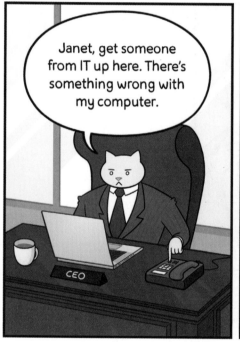

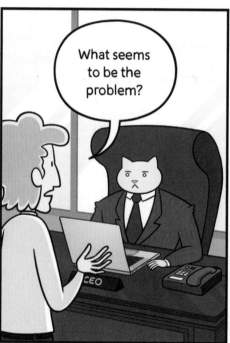

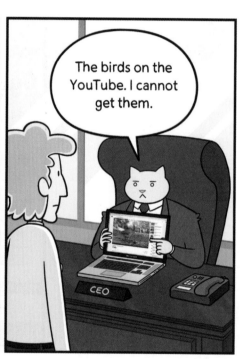

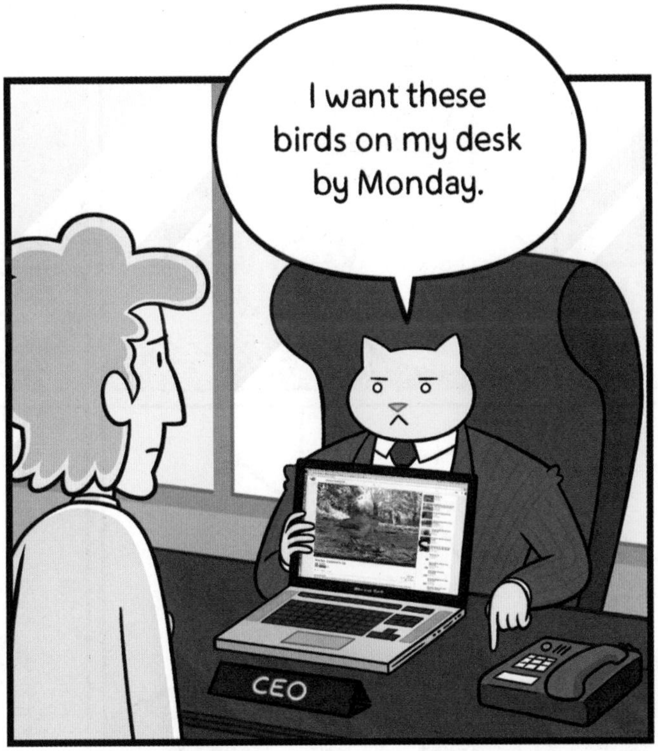
I want these birds on my desk by Monday.
CEO

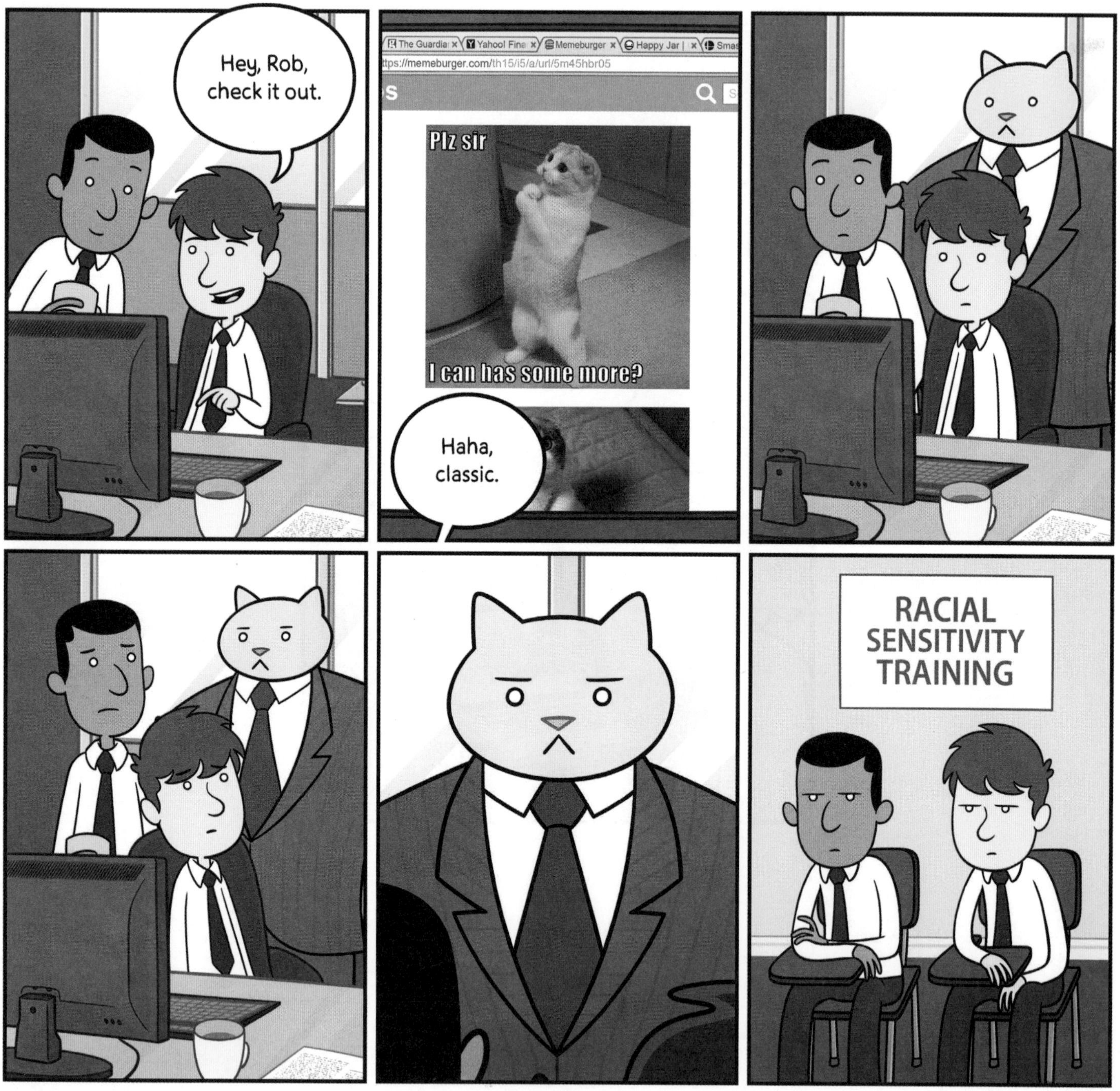
Hey, Rob, check it out.
The Guardia
Yahoo! Fina
Memeburger
Happy Jar
Smas
ttps://memeburger.com/th15/i5/a/url/5m45hbr05
Plz sir
I can has some more?
Haha, classic.
RACIAL SENSITIVITY TRAINING

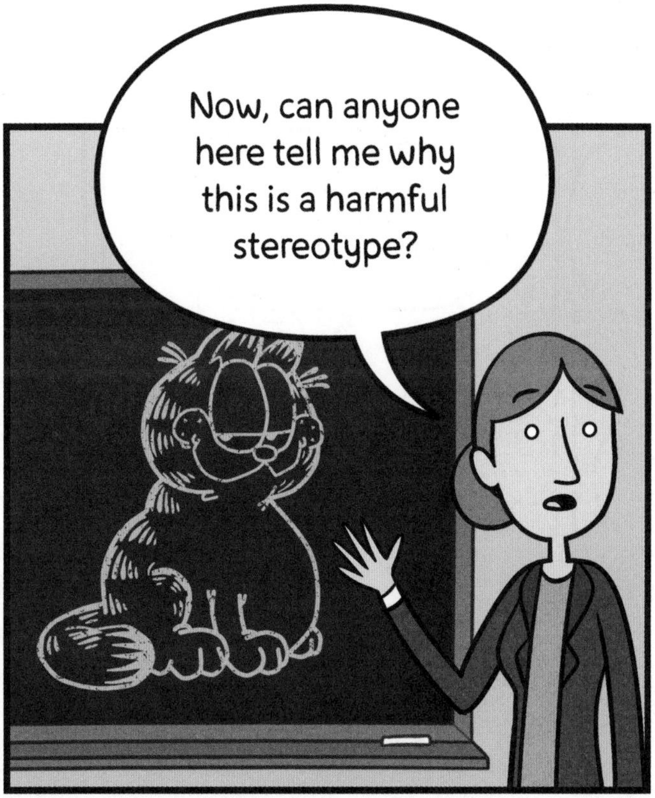
Now, can anyone here tell me why this is a harmful stereotype?

We can't keep meeting like this. People are beginning to talk.
Let them talk.
scratch.
scratch.
scratch.

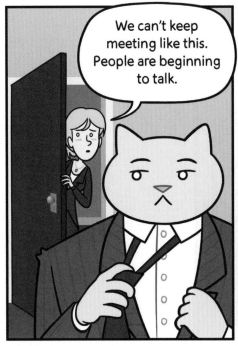

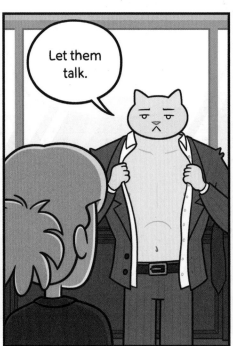

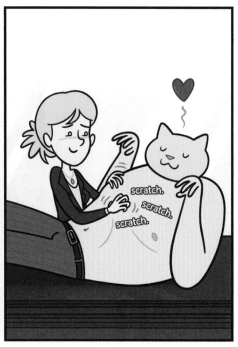

scratch.
scratch.
scratch.
scratch.
scratch.
scratch.
CHOMP!
No more.

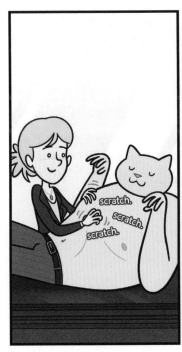

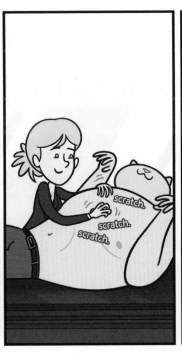

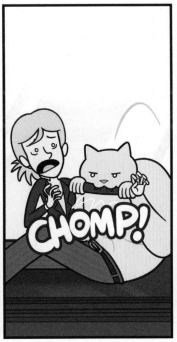

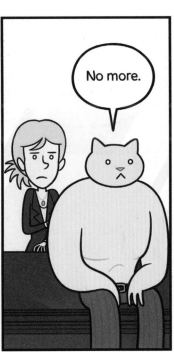

Hey, Janet? Cancel my ten o'clock. I'm going to be late.
Yeah. Yeah, it happened again.

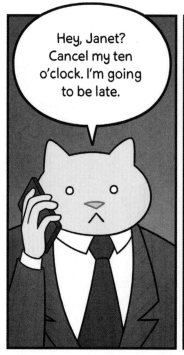

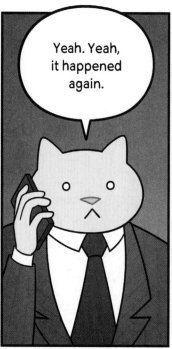

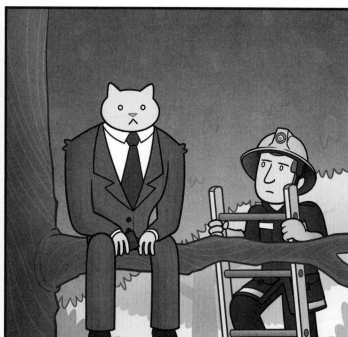

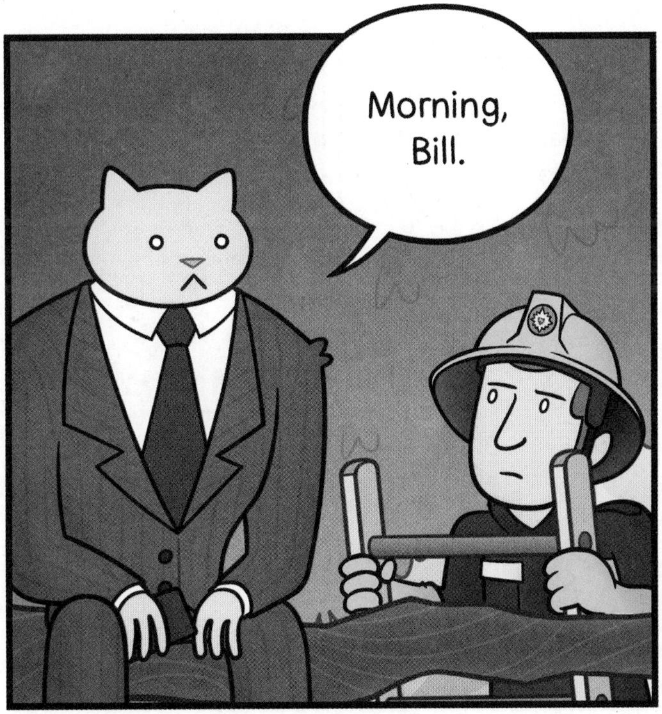
Morning, Bill.

So, in this folder I've got your presentation notes, list of contacts, entry passes, hotel reservations, and anything else you might need for the big conference this weekend.

Great. Thanks, Janet.

Ready to hit the road?

Ready.

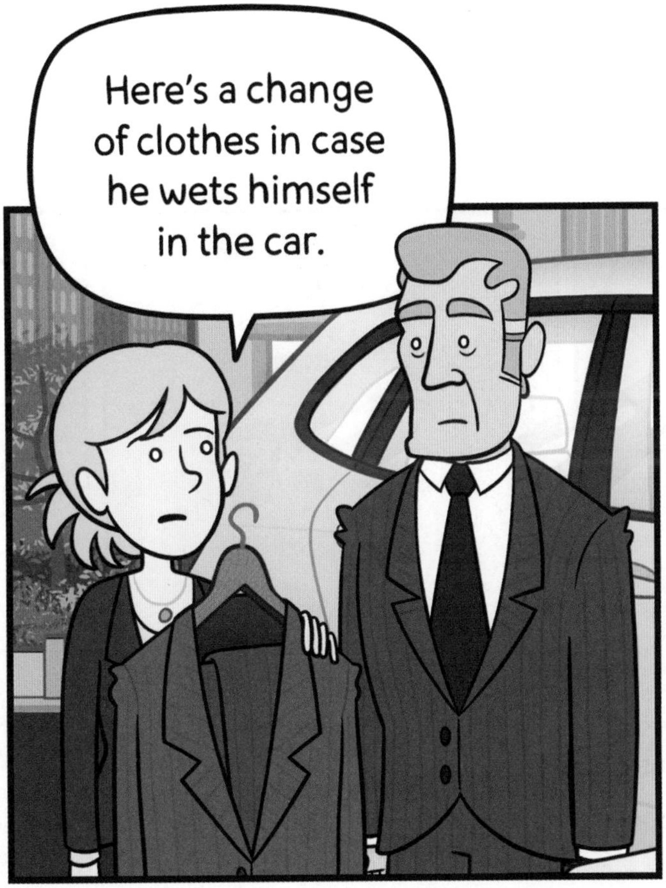
Here's a change of clothes in case he wets himself in the car.

Okay, so I spoke with reception and it looks like there's been a mix-up. We're going to have to share a room.
Um, wow. Okay.
Just so you know, everything with urine on it is mine.

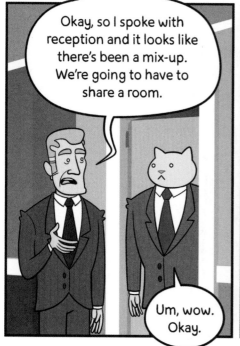

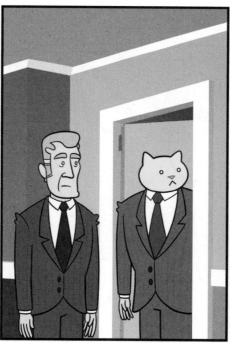

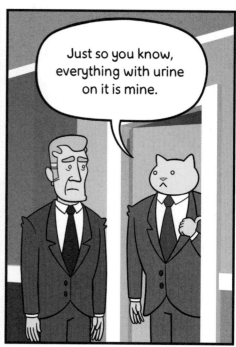

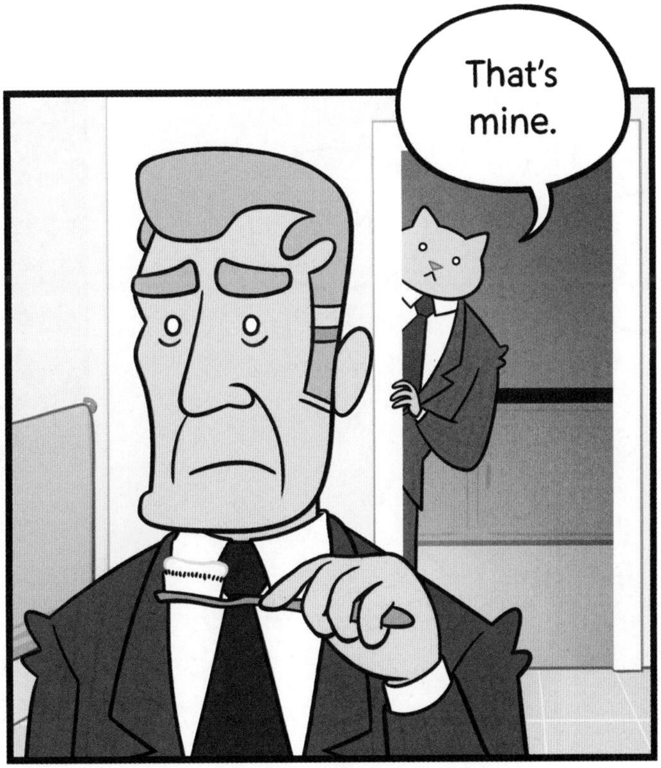
That's mine.

All right, time to pack it in. We've got a big day tomorrow.
Yeah, okay.
Night.
Night.

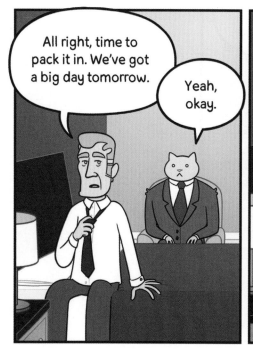

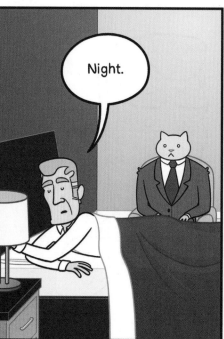

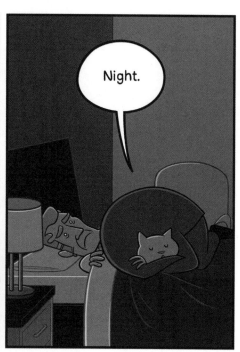

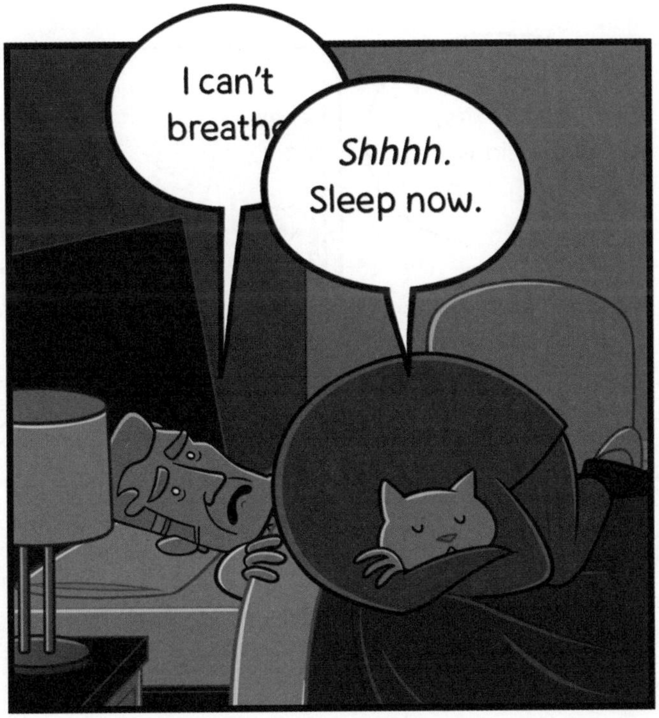
I can't breath
Shhhh. Sleep now.

All right, time to network. There are some powerful people in this room.
Here, put this on. First impressions are everything.

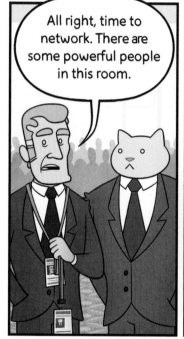

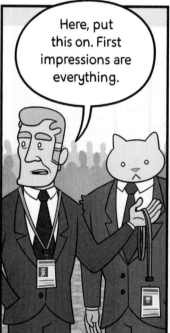

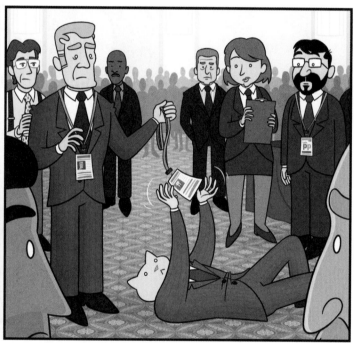

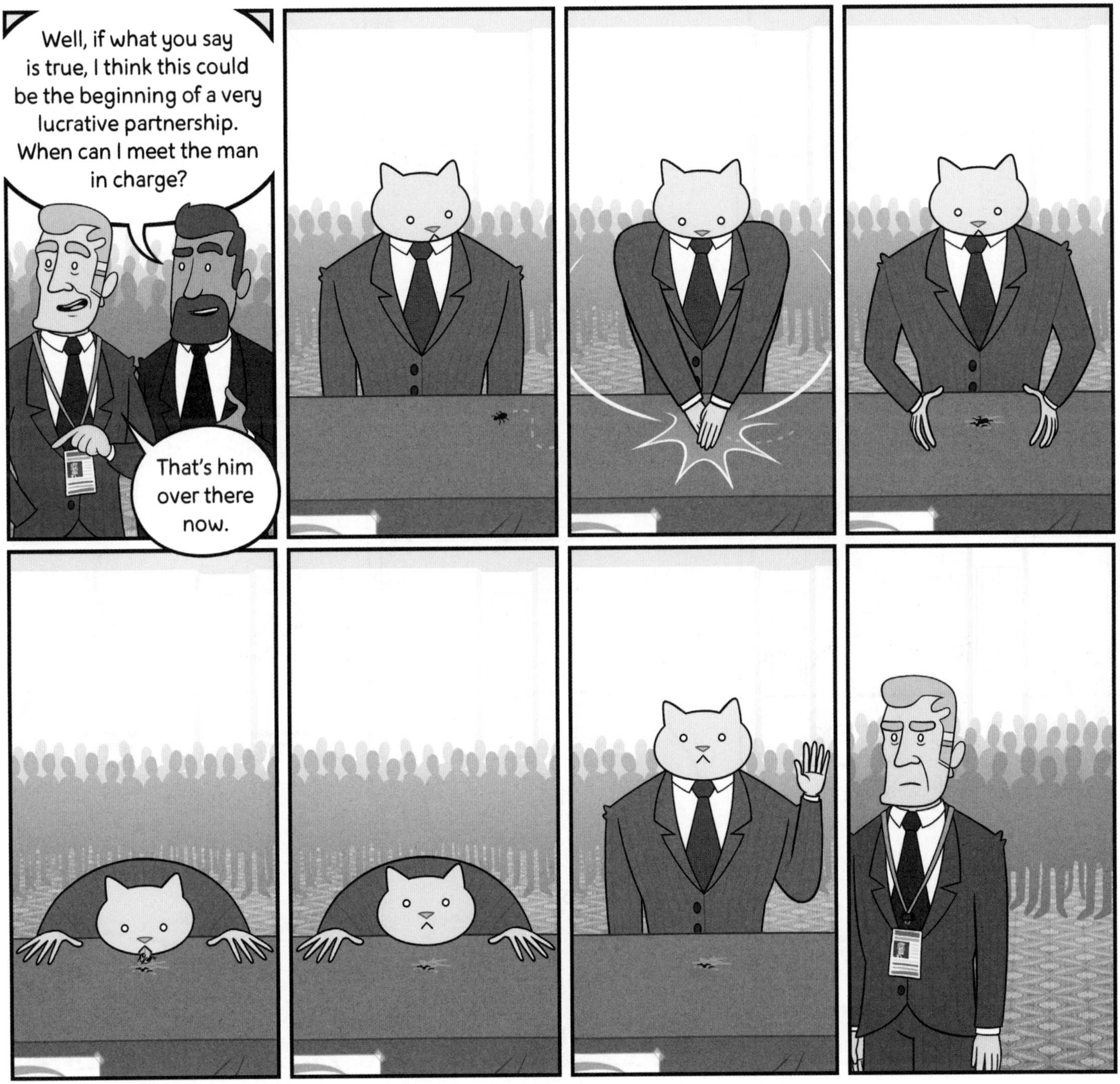
Well, if what you say is true, I think this could be the beginning of a very lucrative partnership. When can I meet the man in charge?
That's him over there now.

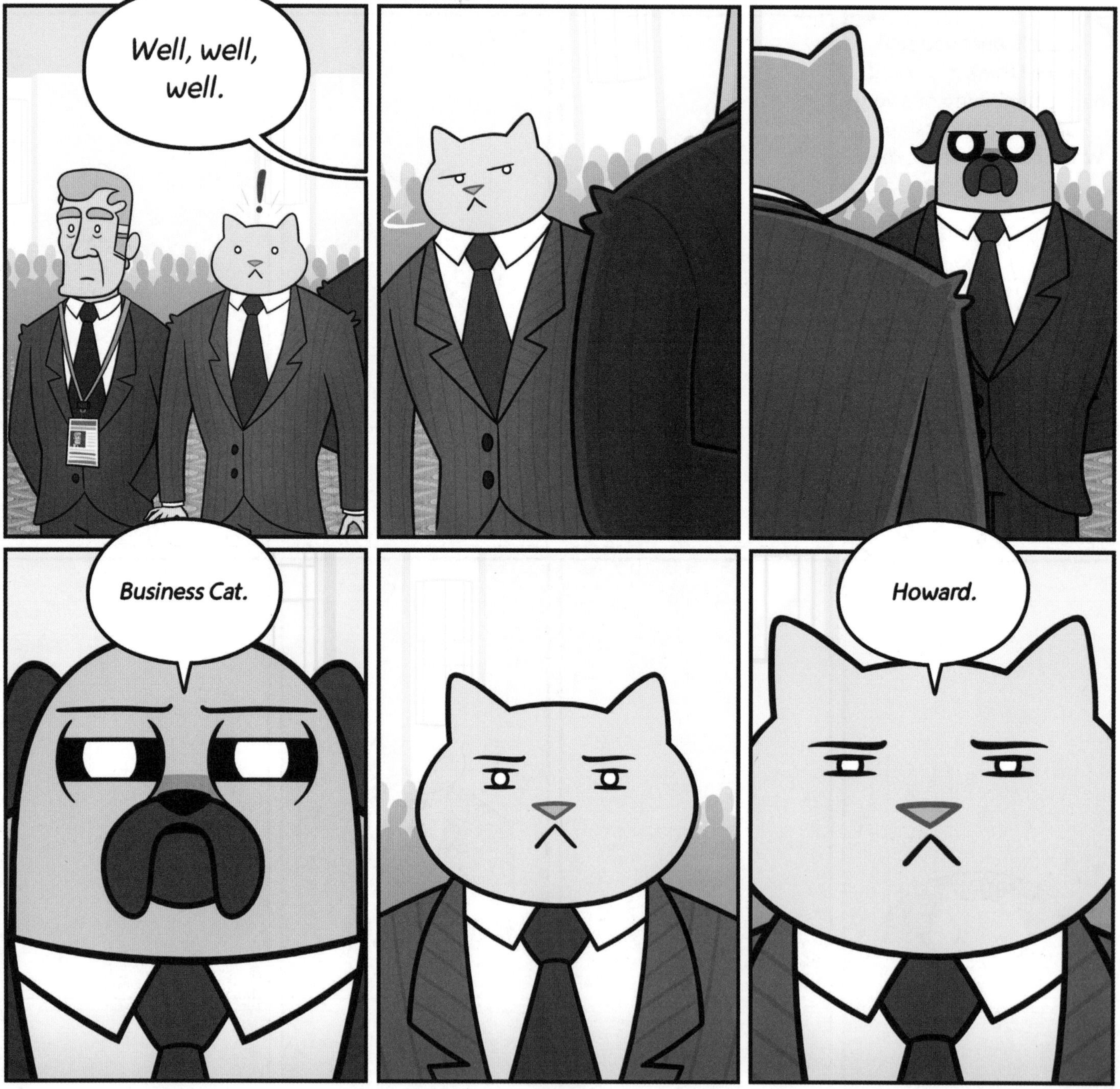
Well, well,
well.
!
Business Cat.
Howard.

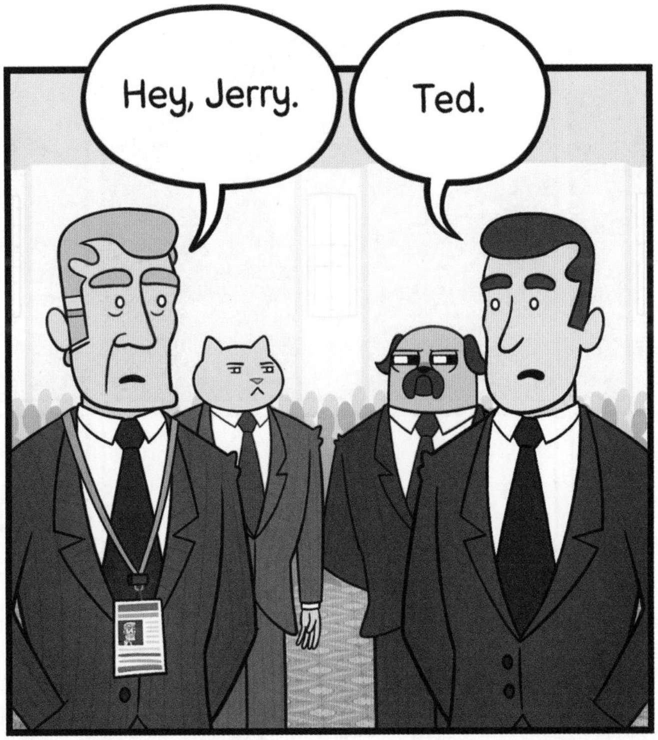
Hey, Jerry.
Ted.

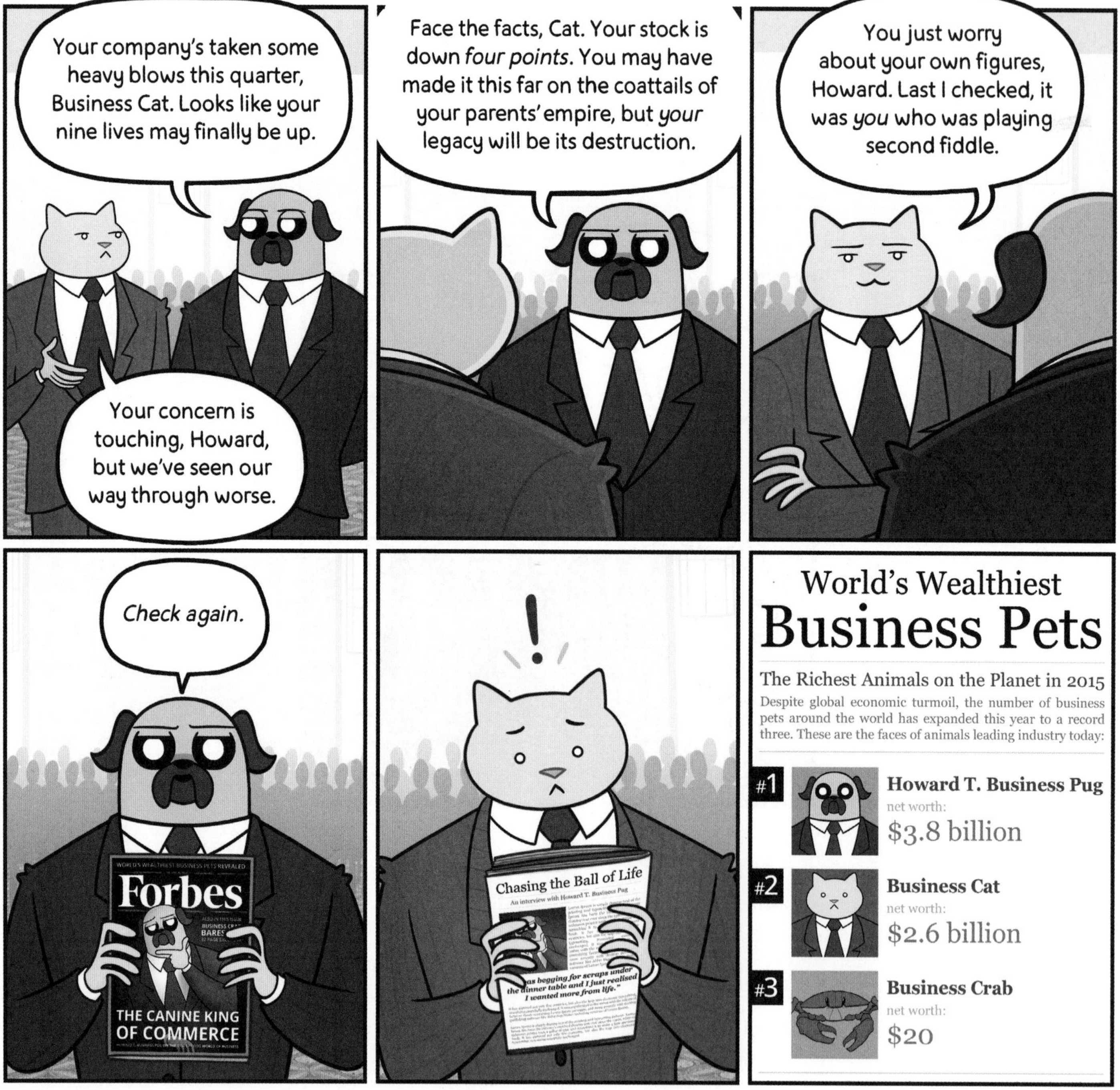
Your company's taken some heavy blows this quarter, Business Cat. Looks like your nine lives may finally be up.
Your concern is touching, Howard, but we've seen our way through worse.
Face the facts, Cat. Your stock is down *four points*. You may have made it this far on the coattails of your parents' empire, but *your* legacy will be its destruction.
You just worry about your own figures, Howard. Last I checked, it was *you* who was playing second fiddle.
Check again.
WORLD'S WEALTHIEST BUSINESS PETS REVEALED
Forbes
THE CANINE KING OF COMMERCE
!
Chasing the Ball of Life
An interview with Howard T. Business Pug
I wanted more from life."
World's Wealthiest
Business Pets
The Richest Animals on the Planet in 2015
Despite global economic turmoil, the number of business pets around the world has expanded this year to a record three. These are the faces of animals leading industry today:
#1
Howard T. Business Pug
net worth:
$3.8 billion
#2
Business Cat
net worth:
$2.6 billion
#3
Business Crab
net worth:
$20

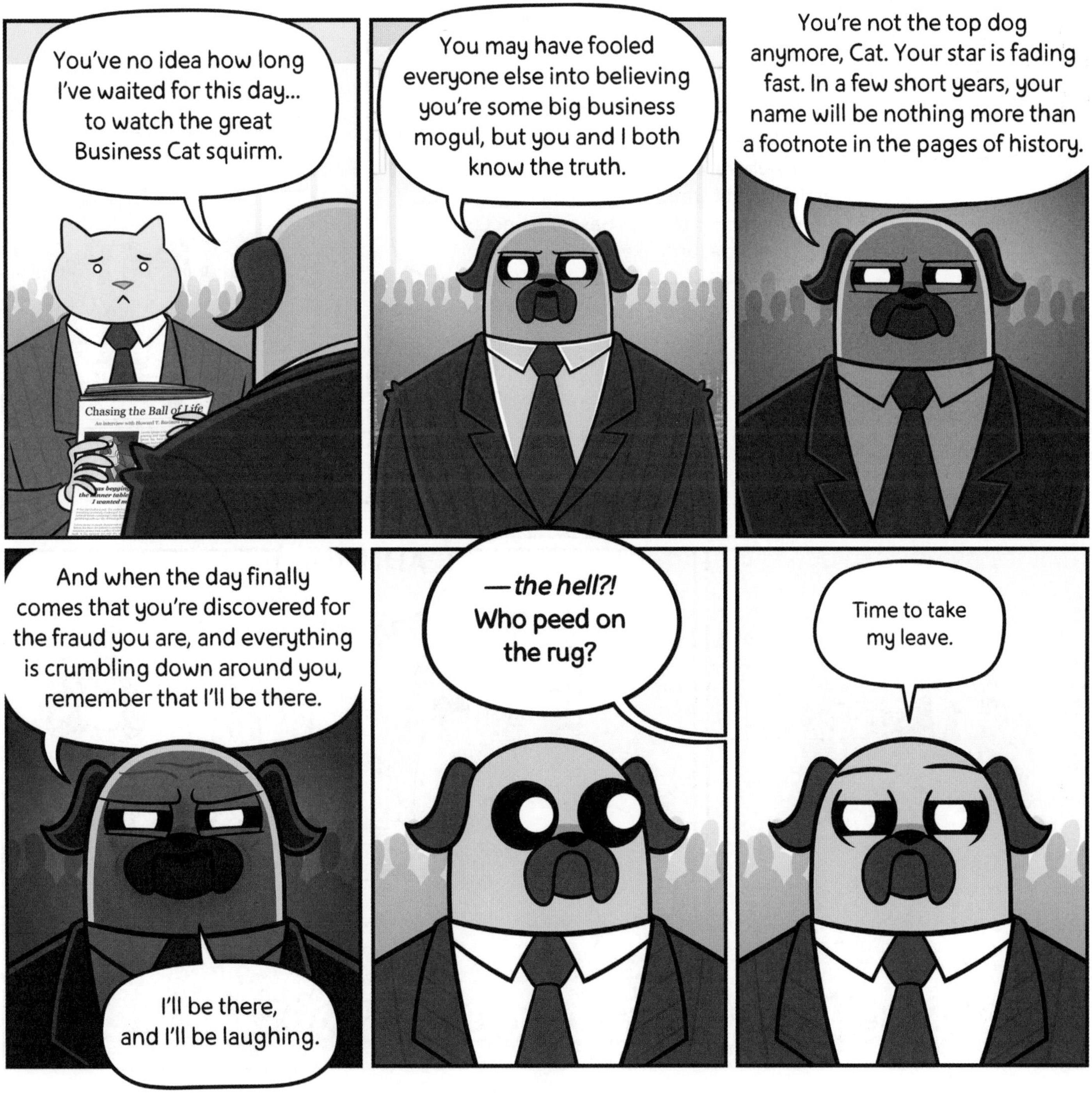
You've no idea how long I've waited for this day... to watch the great Business Cat squirm.
Chasing the Ball of Life
You may have fooled everyone else into believing you're some big business mogul, but you and I both know the truth.
You're not the top dog anymore, Cat. Your star is fading fast. In a few short years, your name will be nothing more than a footnote in the pages of history.
And when the day finally comes that you're discovered for the fraud you are, and everything is crumbling down around you, remember that I'll be there.
I'll be there, and I'll be laughing.
—the hell?! Who peed on the rug?
Time to take my leave.

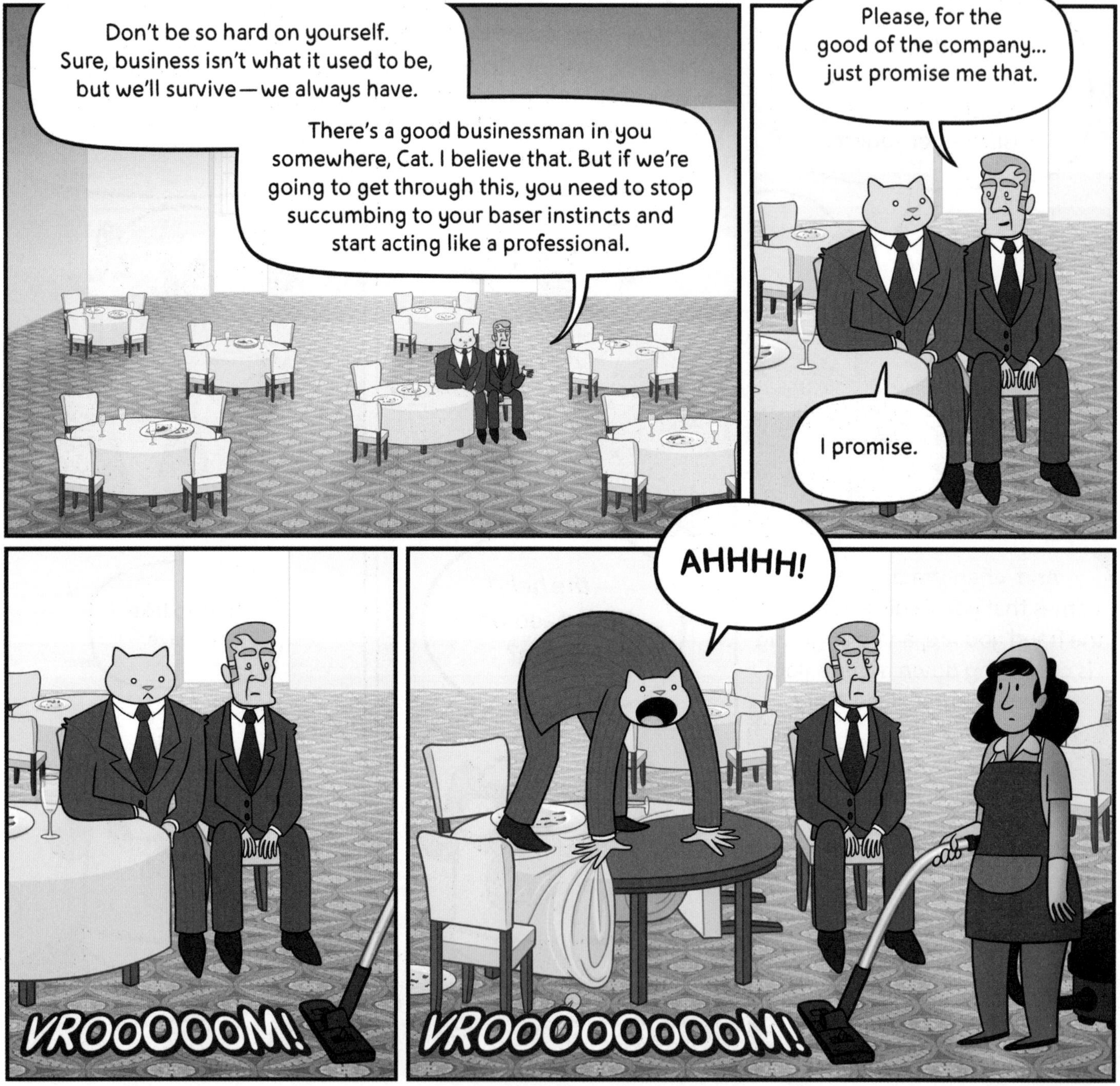
Don't be so hard on yourself. Sure, business isn't what it used to be, but we'll survive—we always have.
There's a good businessman in you somewhere, Cat. I believe that. But if we're going to get through this, you need to stop succumbing to your baser instincts and start acting like a professional.
Please, for the good of the company... just promise me that.
I promise.
VROoOOoOM!
AHHHH!
VROoOOOOoOOoM!

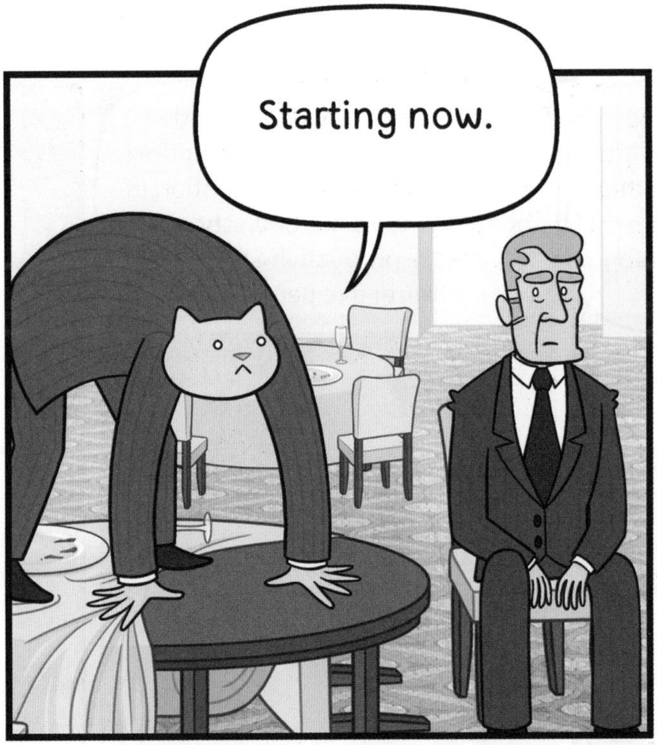
Starting now.

Time and again, studies have shown that *happy* employees are *hardworking* employees. How, then, do we create an office environment conducive to happiness, thereby maximizing profits?
BIZCON
The solution begins with you.
Spend time socializing with your employees—not as their boss, but as their *friend*. Participation in bonding rituals has been shown to increase productivity by up to thirty-five percent.
thwip.
thwip.
thwip.

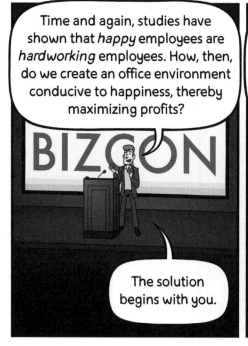

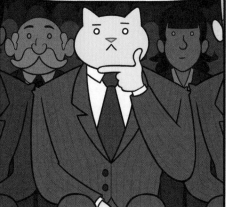

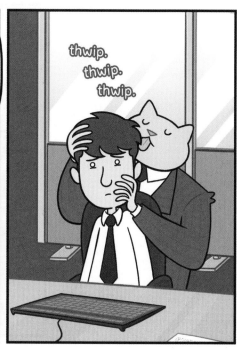

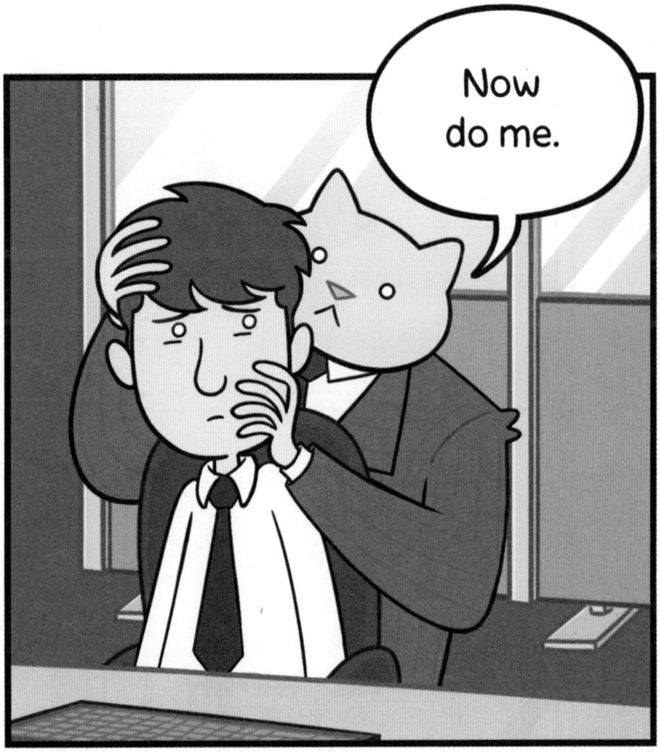
Now do me.

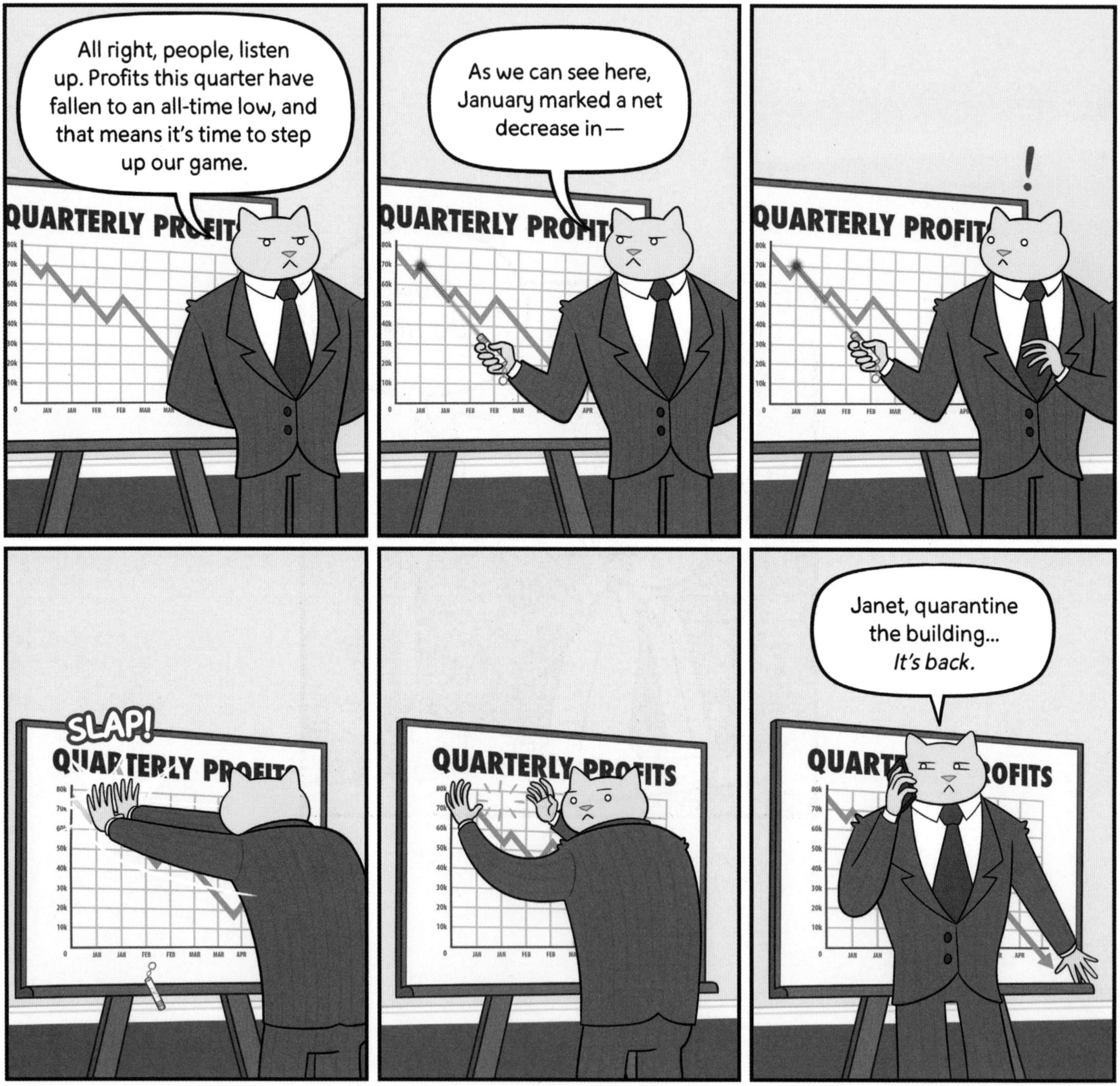

All right, people, listen up. Profits this quarter have fallen to an all-time low, and that means it's time to step up our game.
QUARTERLY PROFITS
As we can see here, January marked a net decrease in—
!
SLAP!
Janet, quarantine the building...
It's back.

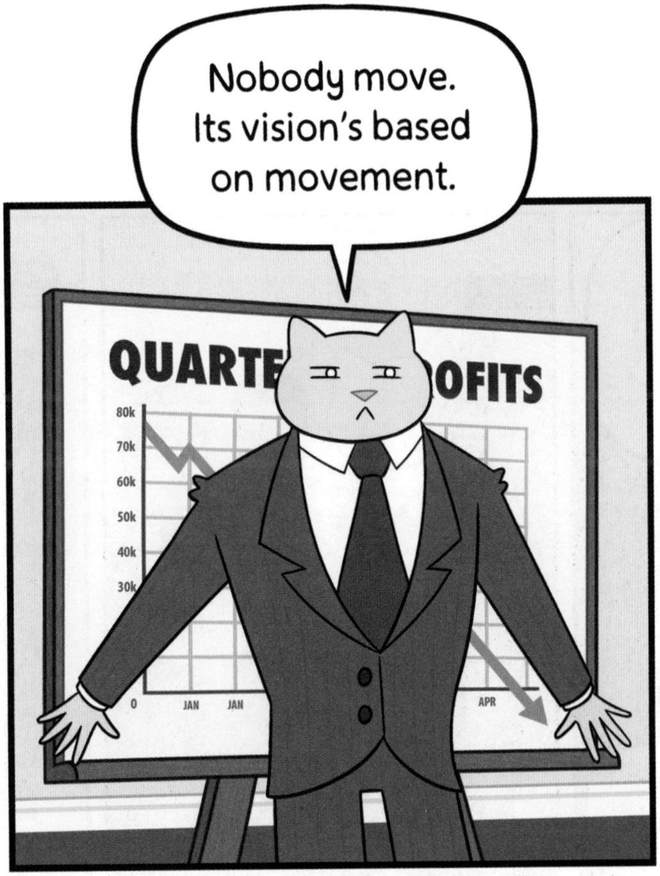
Nobody move.
Its vision's based
on movement.
QUARTE
OFITS
80k
70k
60k
50k
40k
30k
0
JAN
JAN
APR

I've been thinking about ways to boost productivity, and I thought we could start with an employee-of-the-month program to reward hard workers.
I have just the man in mind.
EMPLOYEE OF THE MONTH

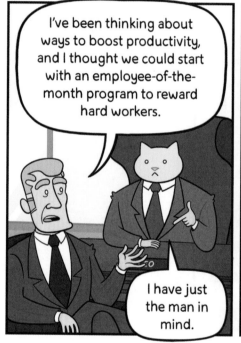

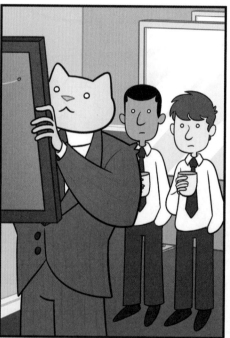

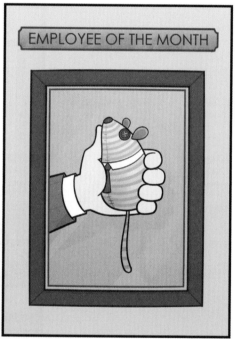

So, I've been going over the accounts and I'm seeing quite a few places we could cut our expenditures.
Hit me.
ACCOUNTANT
Well, for example, it says here under break room budget that we're spending *$2,500* a month on milk and—
No.
But—
The milk stays.
ACCOUNTANT
CEO
MILK

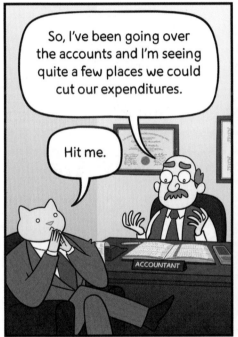

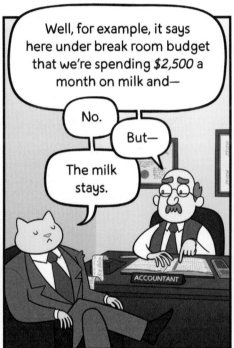

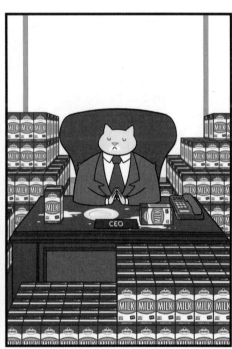

Well, there's no getting around it. If the business is to stay afloat there'll need to be layoffs.
What?! Who?
CEO
Perhaps that other cat who works here.
CEO
Sit down, Jared. We need to talk.

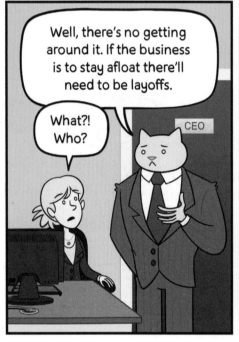

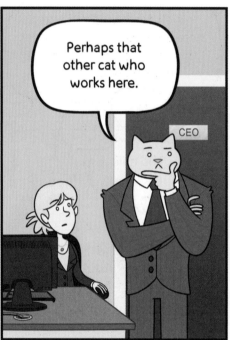

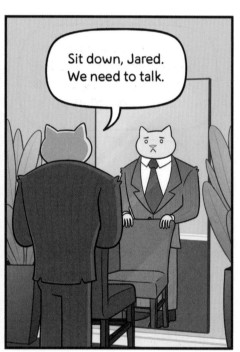

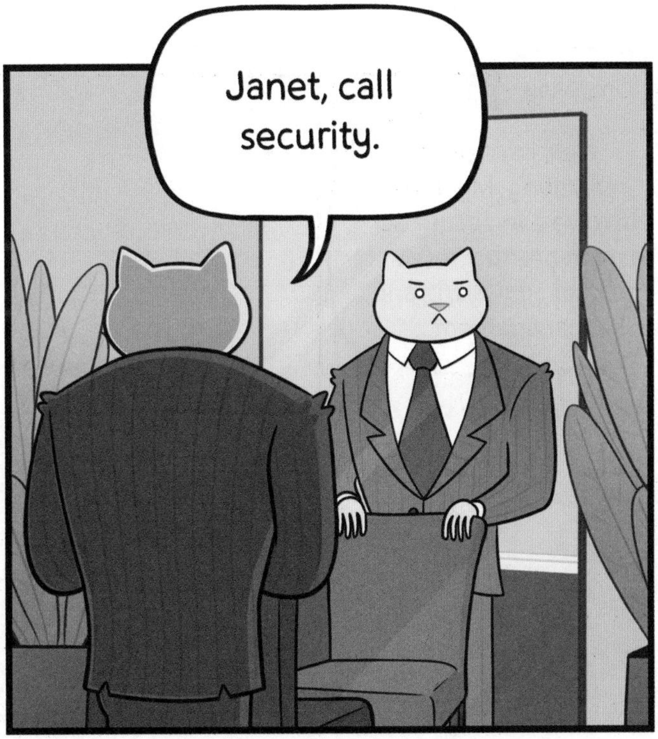
Janet, call security.

Now, I don't want to worry you too much, but we *are* having to make some cuts. I'm just doing the rounds to assess who is and is not essential personnel. So please, run me through what it is you do here.
Um, okay.
Well, I'm head of marketing. My duties involve overseeing our team in product research, market analysis, brand management...
CEO
I also refill your food bowl when Janet's away.
Damn fine work.

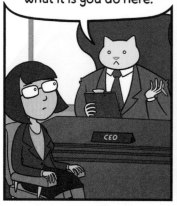

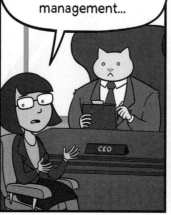

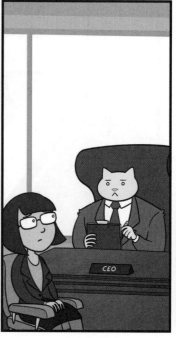

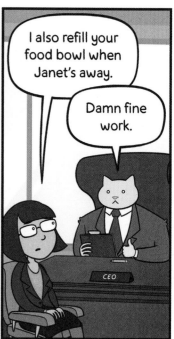

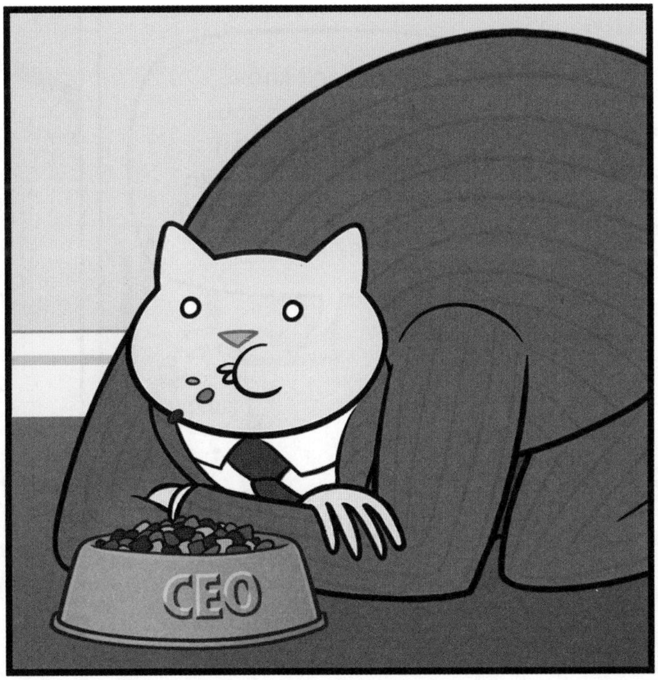
CEO

You've gone through the entire building and there's not a *single* staff member we can afford to let go?
They're all essential. Janet gives me scratches, Mae does my food bowl, Rob changes the litter, and the rest have warm laps to sit on.
ACCOUNTANT
Well, I don't know what else to tell you. There's *no way* I can balance these books with the current number of staff. *Someone* has to go.
ACCOUNTANT
FIND YOUR NEXT JOB ONLINE
jobsearch
*JobSearch reserves the right to 15% of any and all pay checks collected on work found via the JobSearch platform.

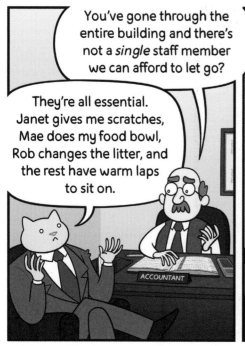

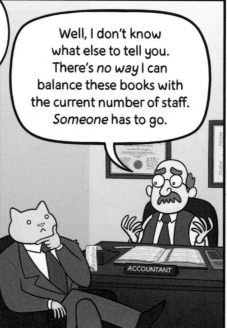

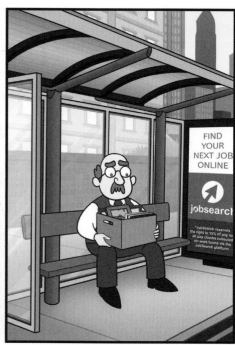

Hold the elevator!

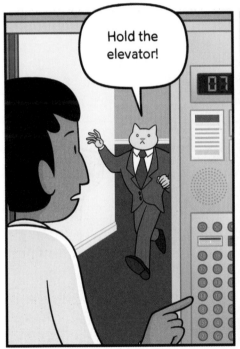

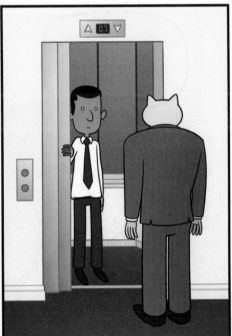

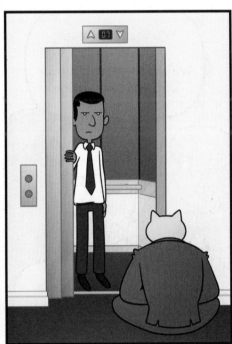

You should probably take a look at this. We've received a claim for wrongful termination.
Sounds more like legal's department. Take it to Gerald.
CEO
I'm not going to take it to Gerald.
Go see Gerald.

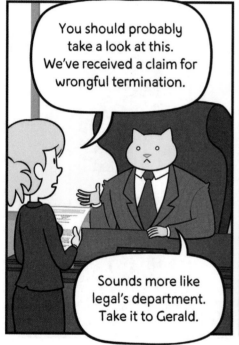

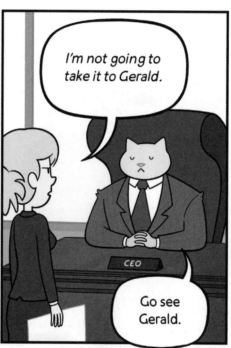

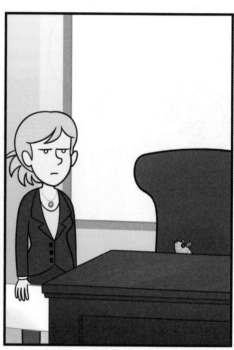

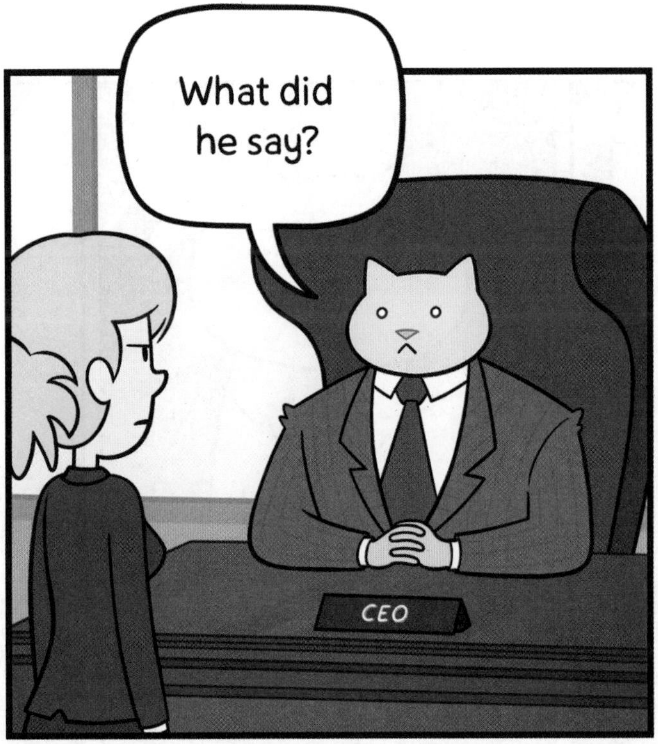
What did he say?
CEO

Uh oh, a black cat crossing our path. That's bad luck, you know.
RACIAL SENSITIVITY TRAINING

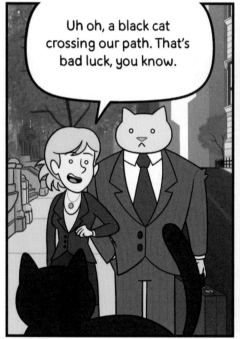

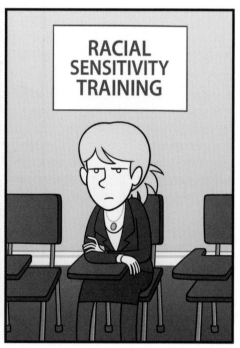

You've got lunch with the investors at two. Want me to drop by your place and pick up a fresh suit for you?
CEO
That won't be necessary.
CEO
CEO

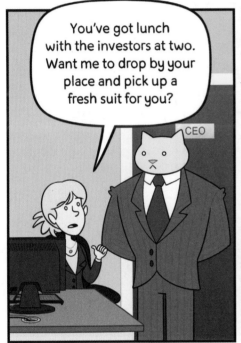

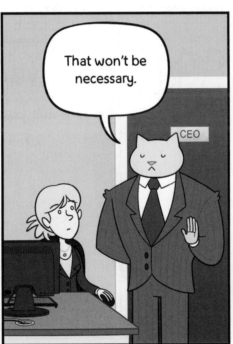

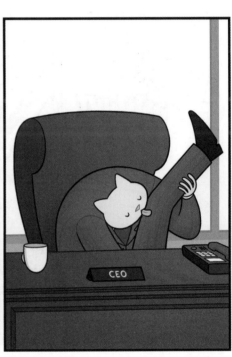

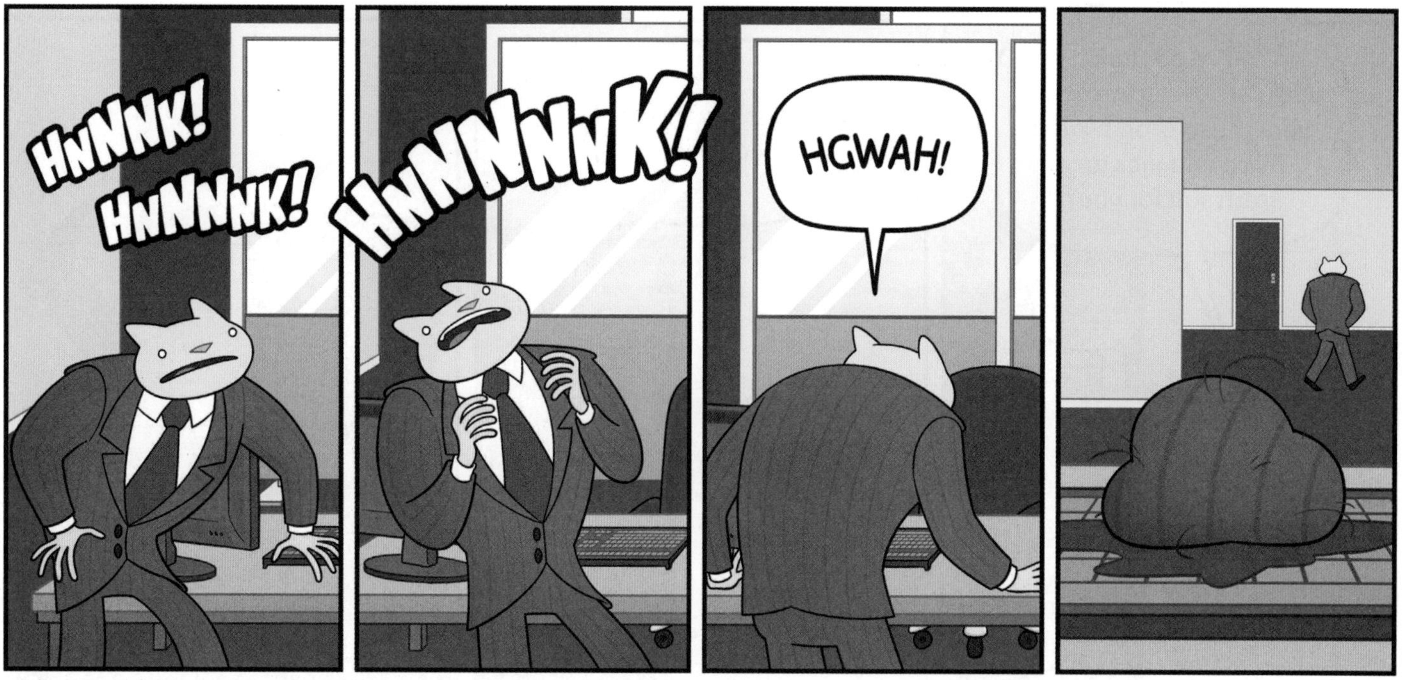
HNNNK!
HNNNNK!
HNNNNNNK!!
HGWAH!

Thank you for joining us, gentlemen. The food here is to die for.
The usual, Mr. C?
Please.

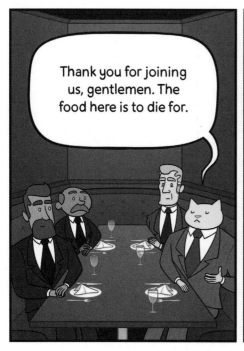

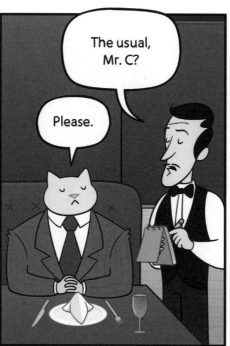

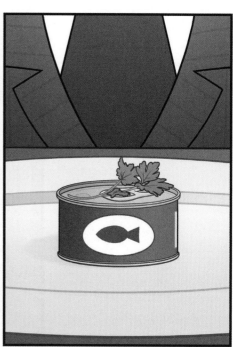

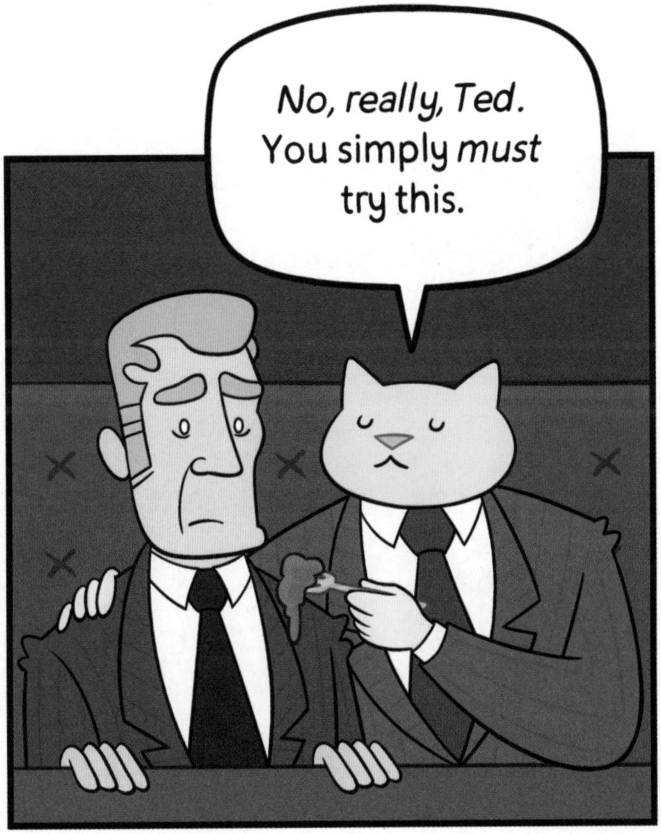
No, really, Ted. You simply *must* try this.

Well, if you ask me, this partnership sounds like cause for celebration.
Agreed.
Waiter, a carton of white for the table.
Mm. Good year.
MILK

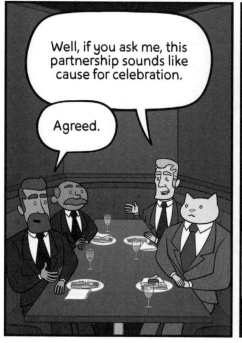

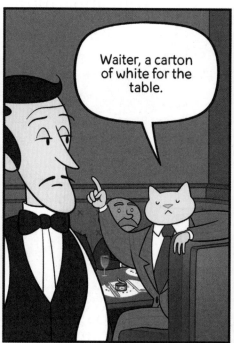

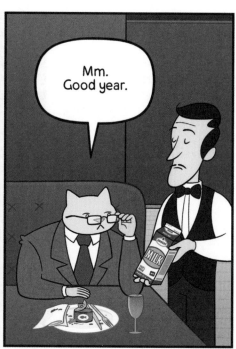

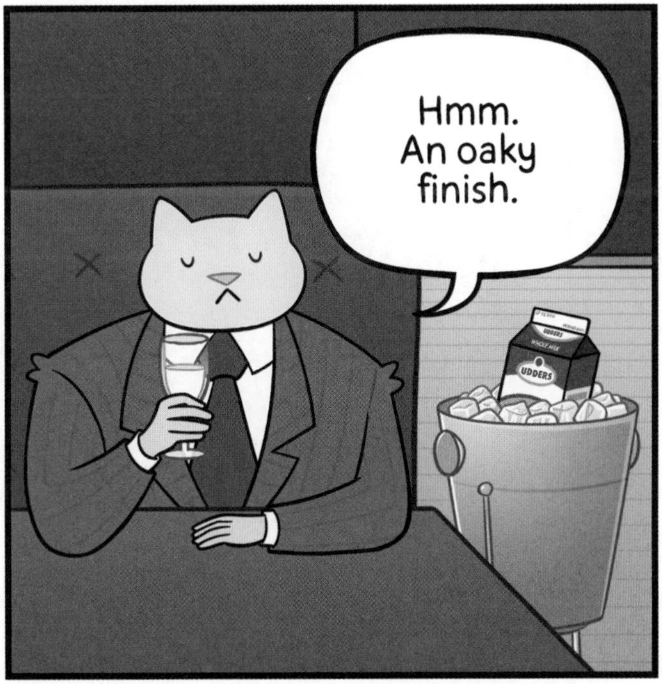
Hmm.
An oaky
finish.
UDDERS

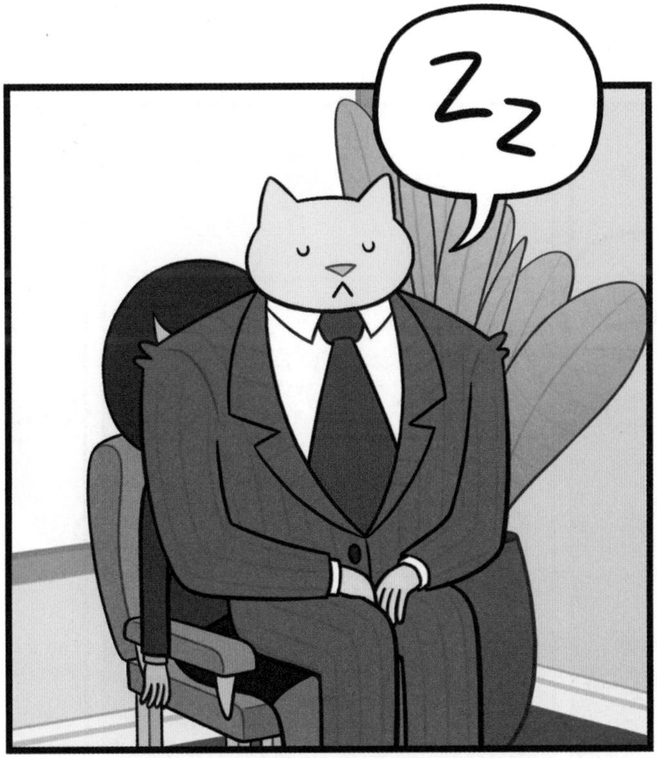
Zz

Janet says you've been having some computer troubles?
Yeah, there's some kind of weird bug in it.
CEO

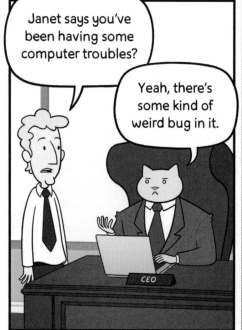

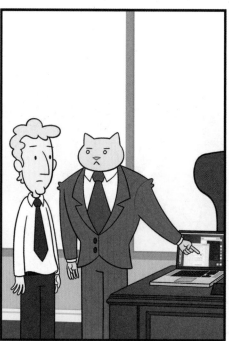

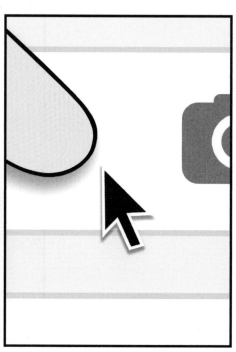

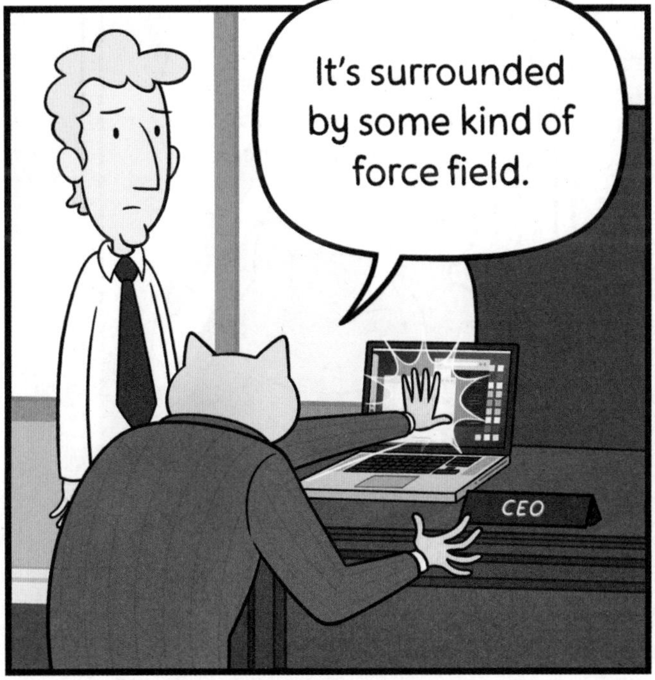
It's surrounded by some kind of force field.
CEO

I just don't know what to do with you anymore, Michaels. You're insubordinate, you don't listen, and you seem to be incapable of completing a single task assigned to you!
CEO
I'm afraid there's nowhere left for me to turn. You've been given one too many chances.
It's time to take *drastic action.*
sfft.
sfft.
sfft.

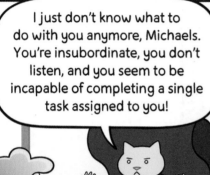

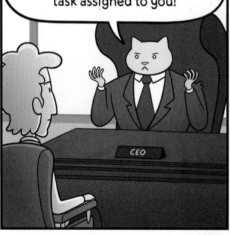

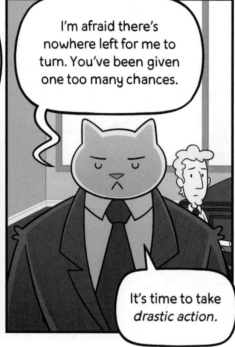

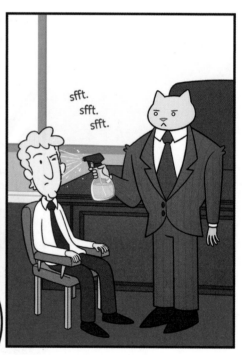

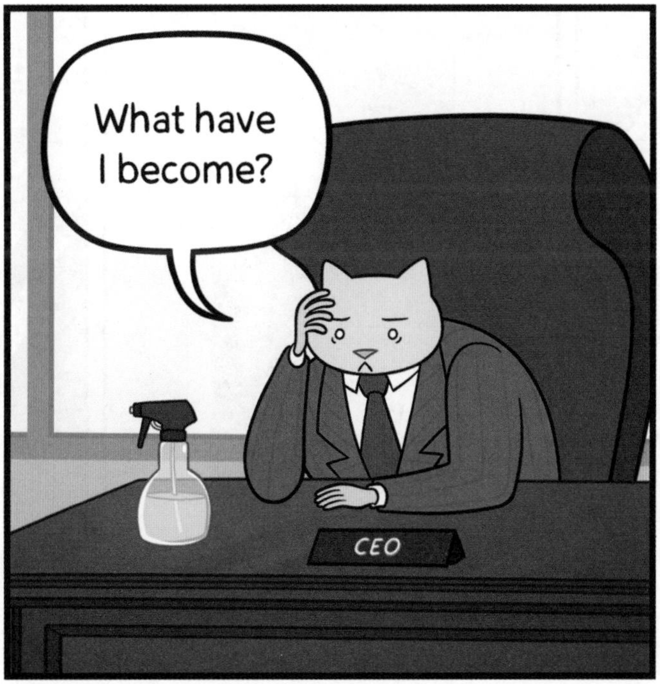
What have I become?
CEO

Janet. Listen. The investors will be here any minute to finalize this deal and I can't risk having *you-know-who* there to screw it all up. Make sure he doesn't leave his office.
Got it.
CEO
EO

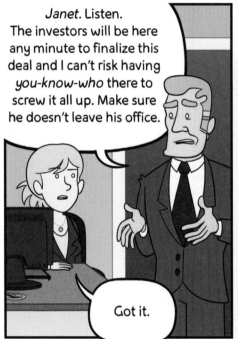

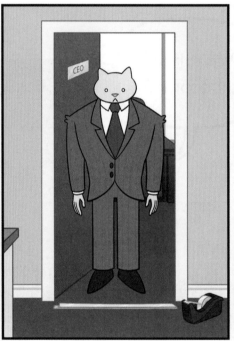

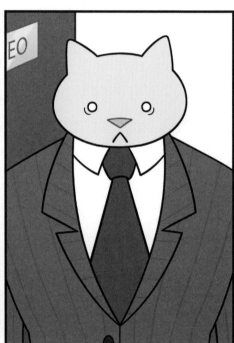

Help.

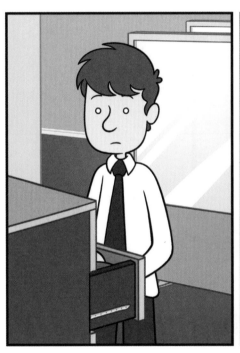

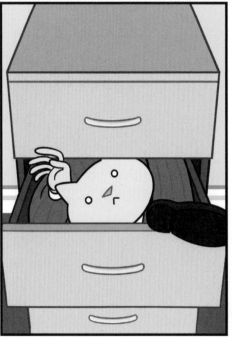

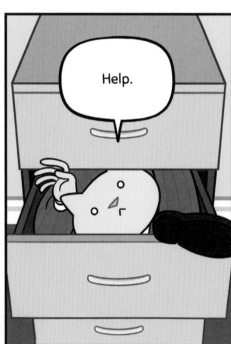

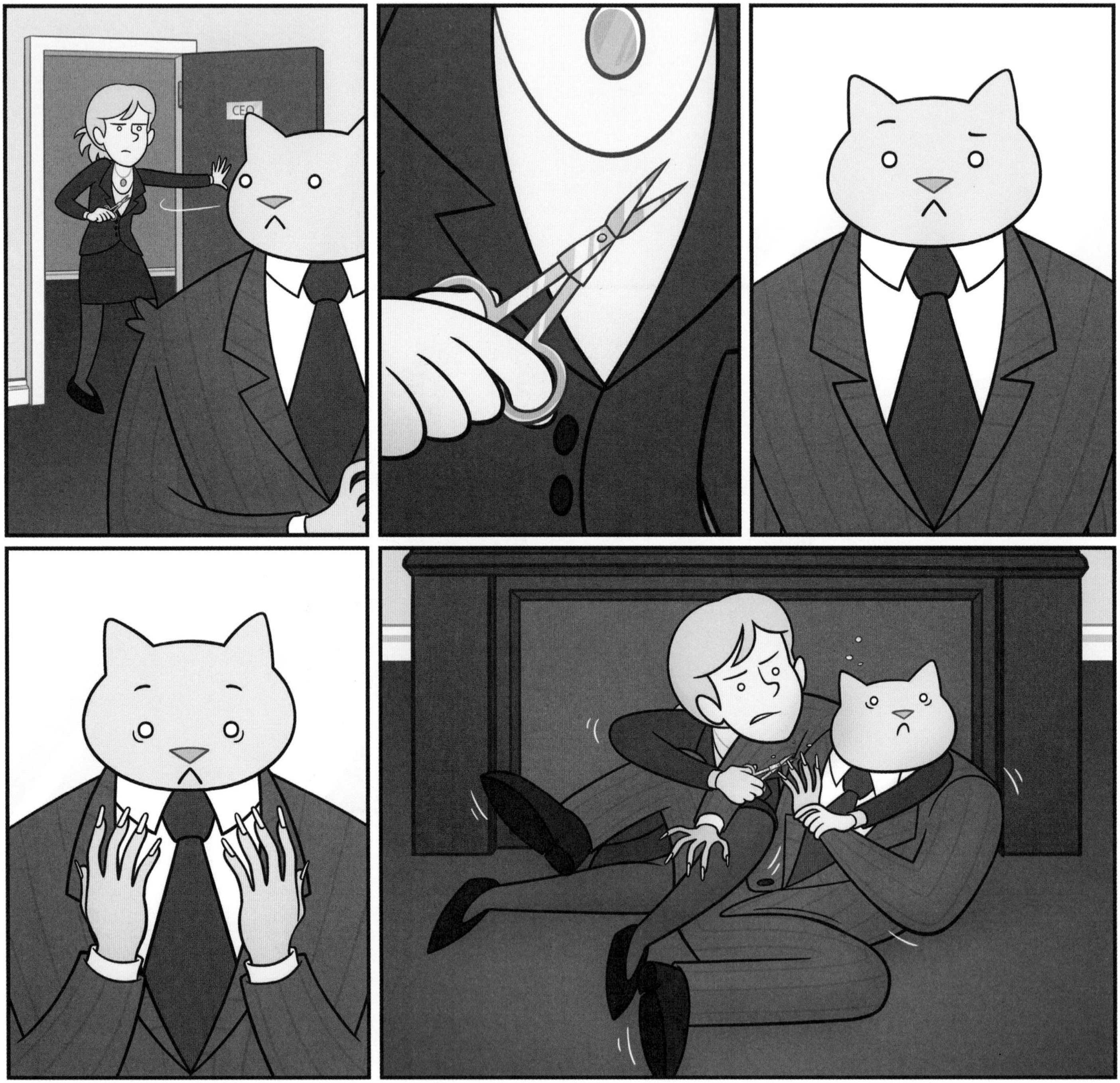
CEO

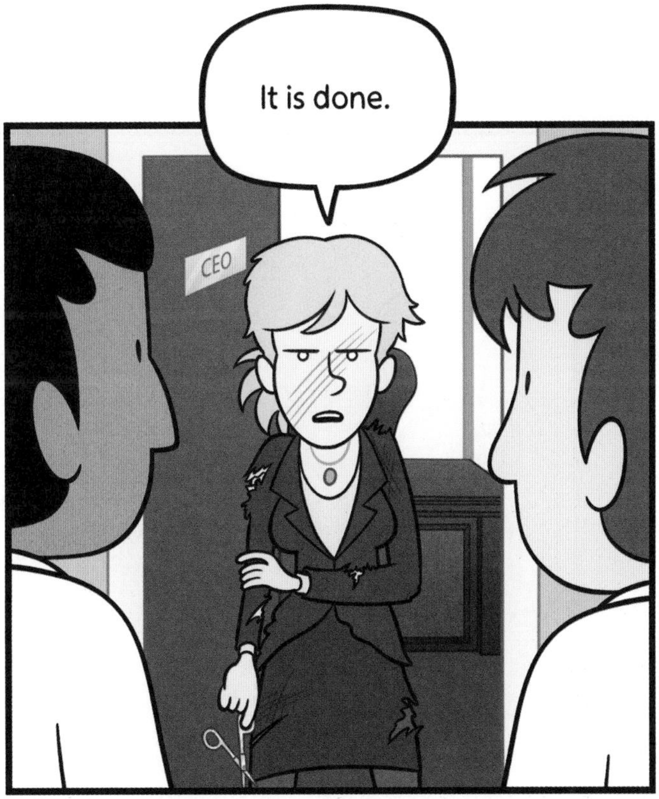
It is done.
CEO

3,678
Inbox
Social
Food.
from: Business Cat 12:03pm
Food time.
from: Business Cat 12:03pm
Time for food.
from: Business Cat 12:02pm
Hey. Need food.
from: Business Cat 12:00pm
Hello?
from: Business Cat 11:58am
Food please.

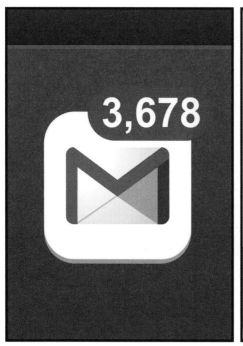

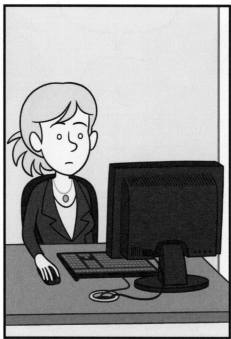

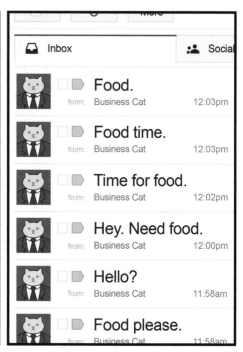

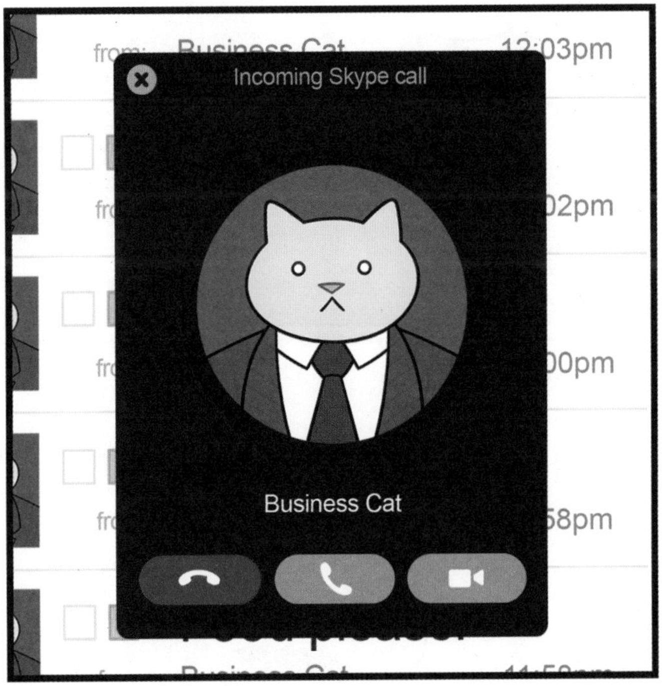
12:03pm
Incoming Skype call
Business Cat

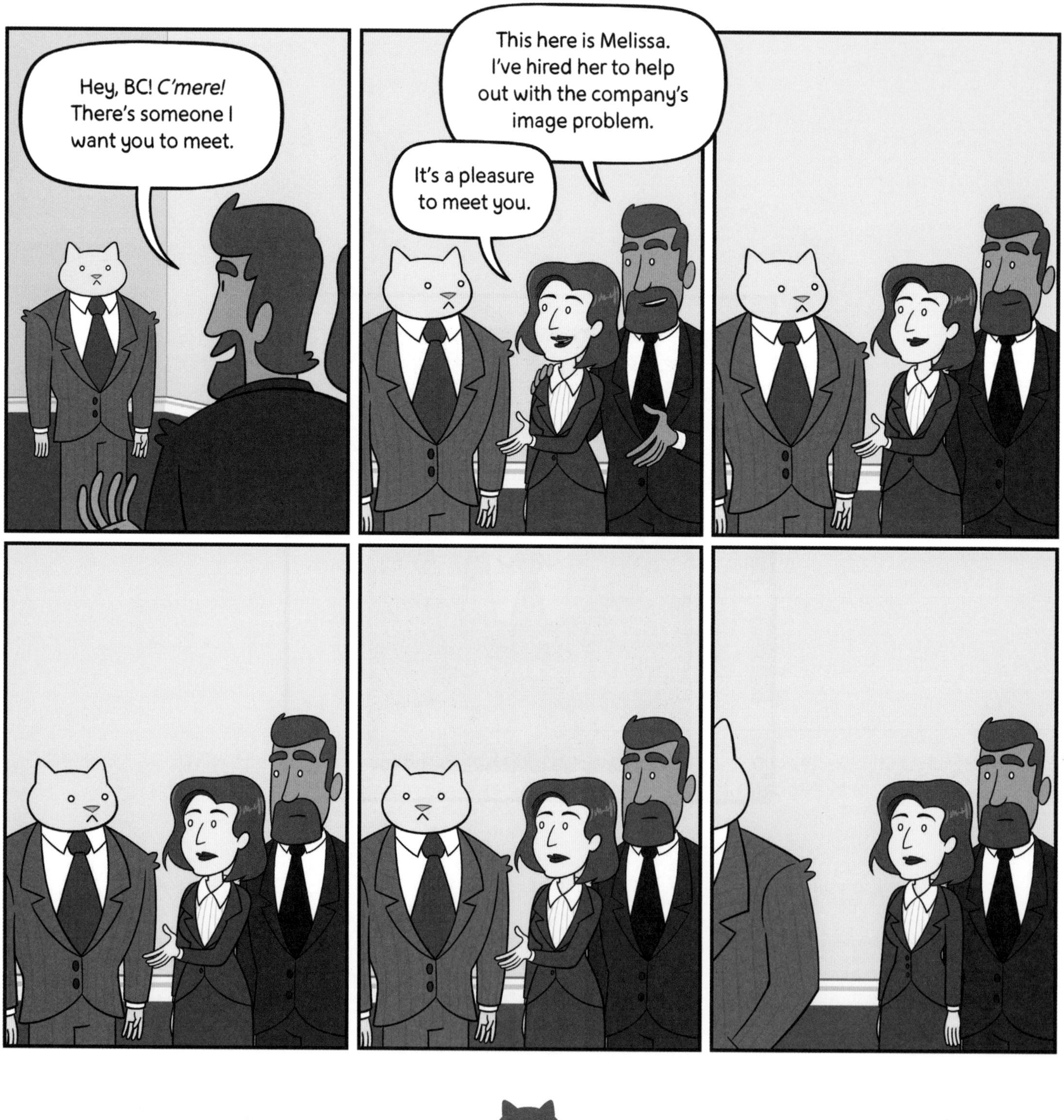
Hey, BC! *C'mere!* There's someone I want you to meet.
This here is Melissa. I've hired her to help out with the company's image problem.
It's a pleasure to meet you.

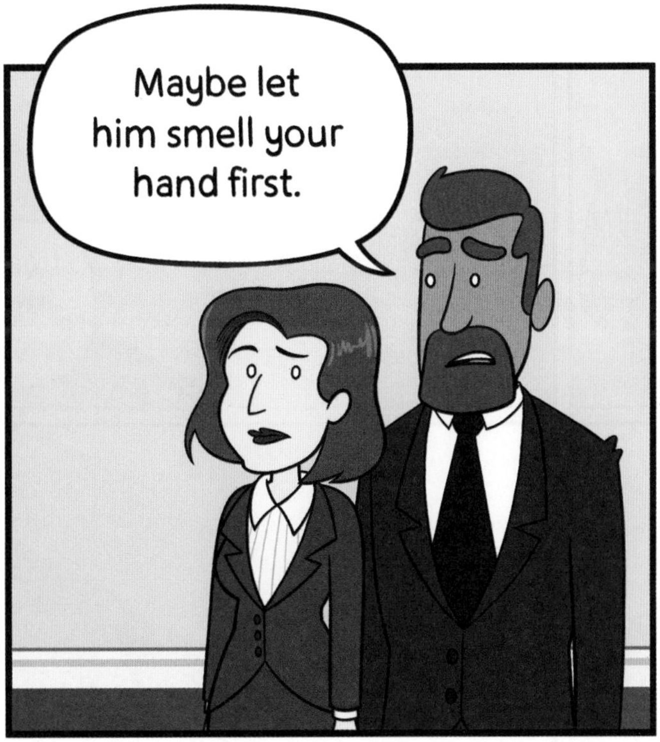
Maybe let him smell your hand first.

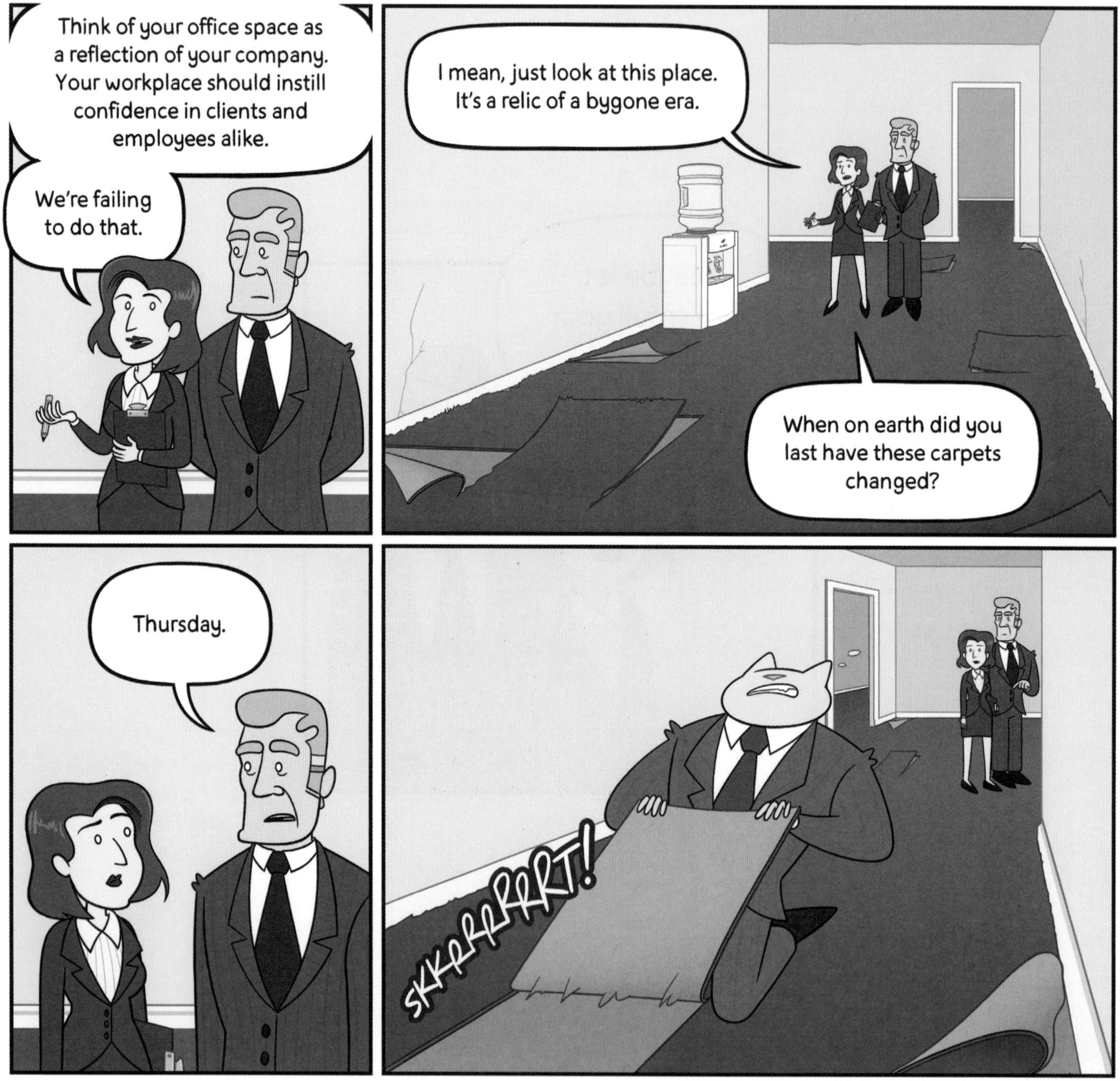
Think of your office space as a reflection of your company. Your workplace should instill confidence in clients and employees alike.
We're failing to do that.
I mean, just look at this place. It's a relic of a bygone era.
When on earth did you last have these carpets changed?
Thursday.
SKRRRRRRT!

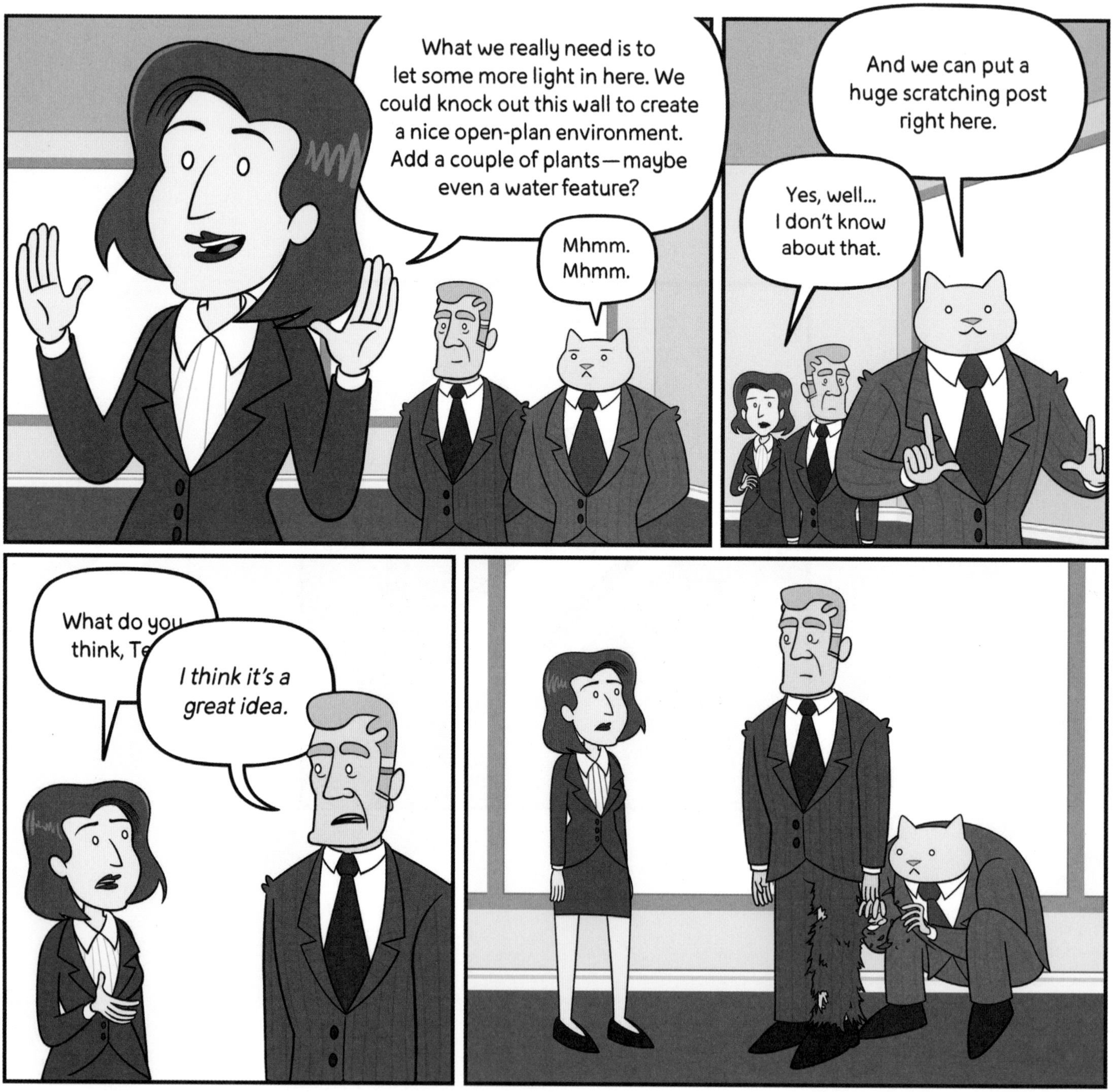
What we really need is to let some more light in here. We could knock out this wall to create a nice open-plan environment. Add a couple of plants—maybe even a water feature?
Mhmm. Mhmm.
And we can put a huge scratching post right here.
Yes, well... I don't know about that.
What do you think, Te
I think it's a great idea.

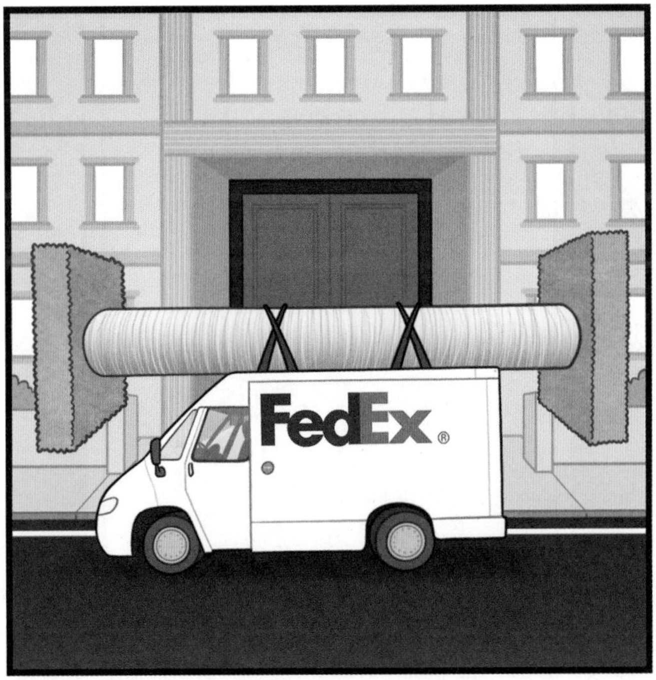
FedEx®

I've got a delivery here for a Mr. Cat?
That's us.
Sign here.
CEO
CEO

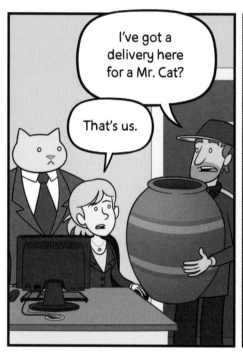

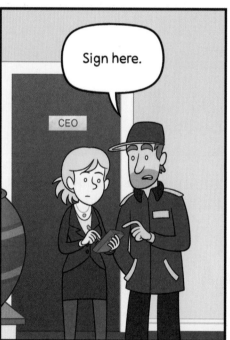

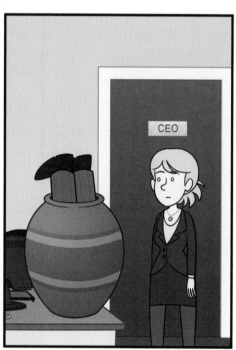

Oh God, sorry about the mess! We've had so many deliveries lately. I'll get it cleaned up as soon as possible.
CEO
No...don't...
It's perfect.

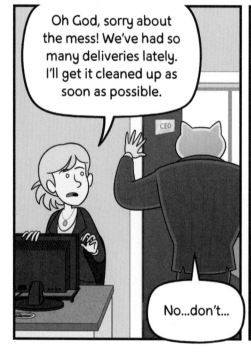

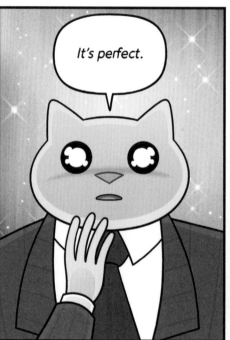

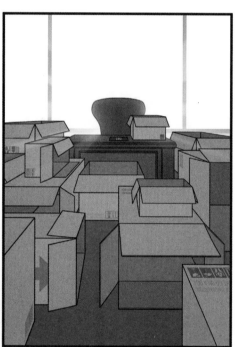

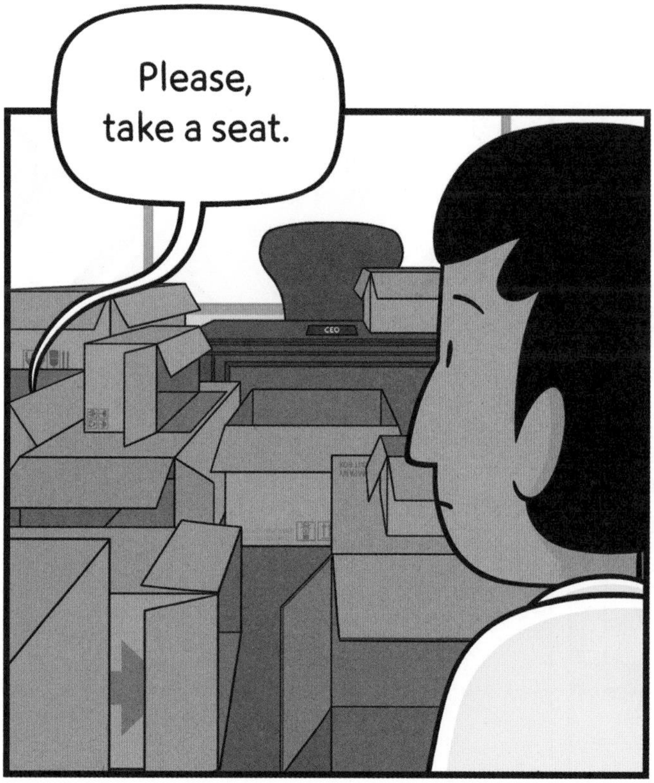
Please, take a seat.

Sorry about all the racket these past few weeks. You guys must be struggling to get any work done with all these renovations going on.
Actually, it's been great. We're getting way more done than usual.
BANG!
SLAM!
SCRAPE!
CRASH!
HAMMER!
NAIL!

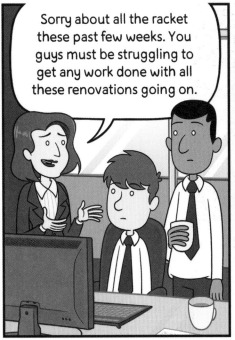

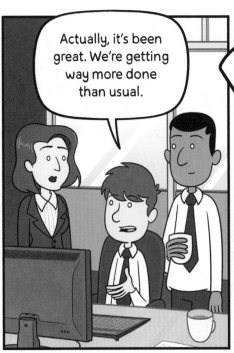

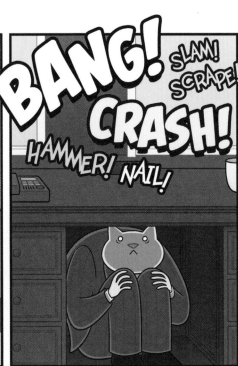

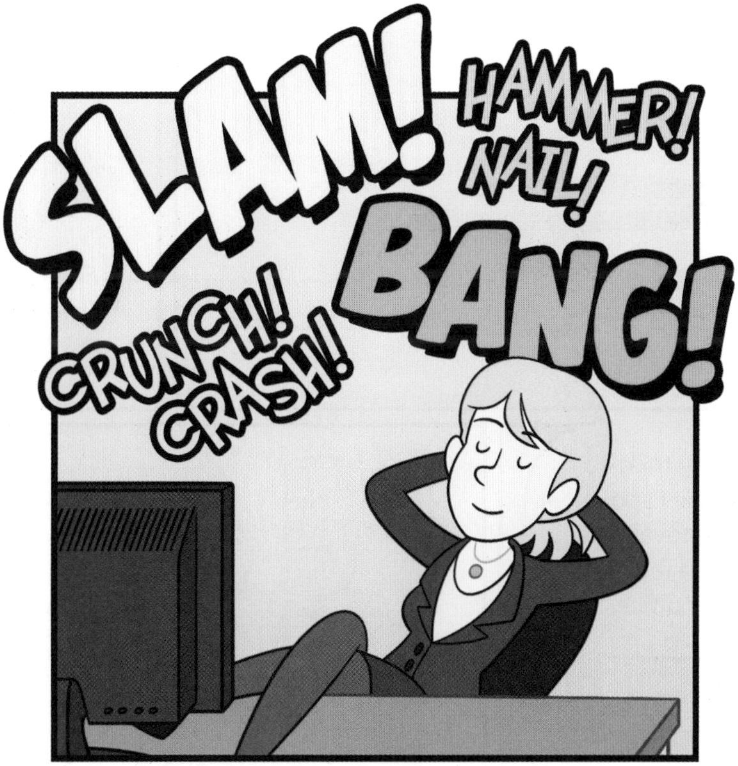
SLAM!
HAMMER!
NAIL!
BANG!
CRUNCH!
CRASH!

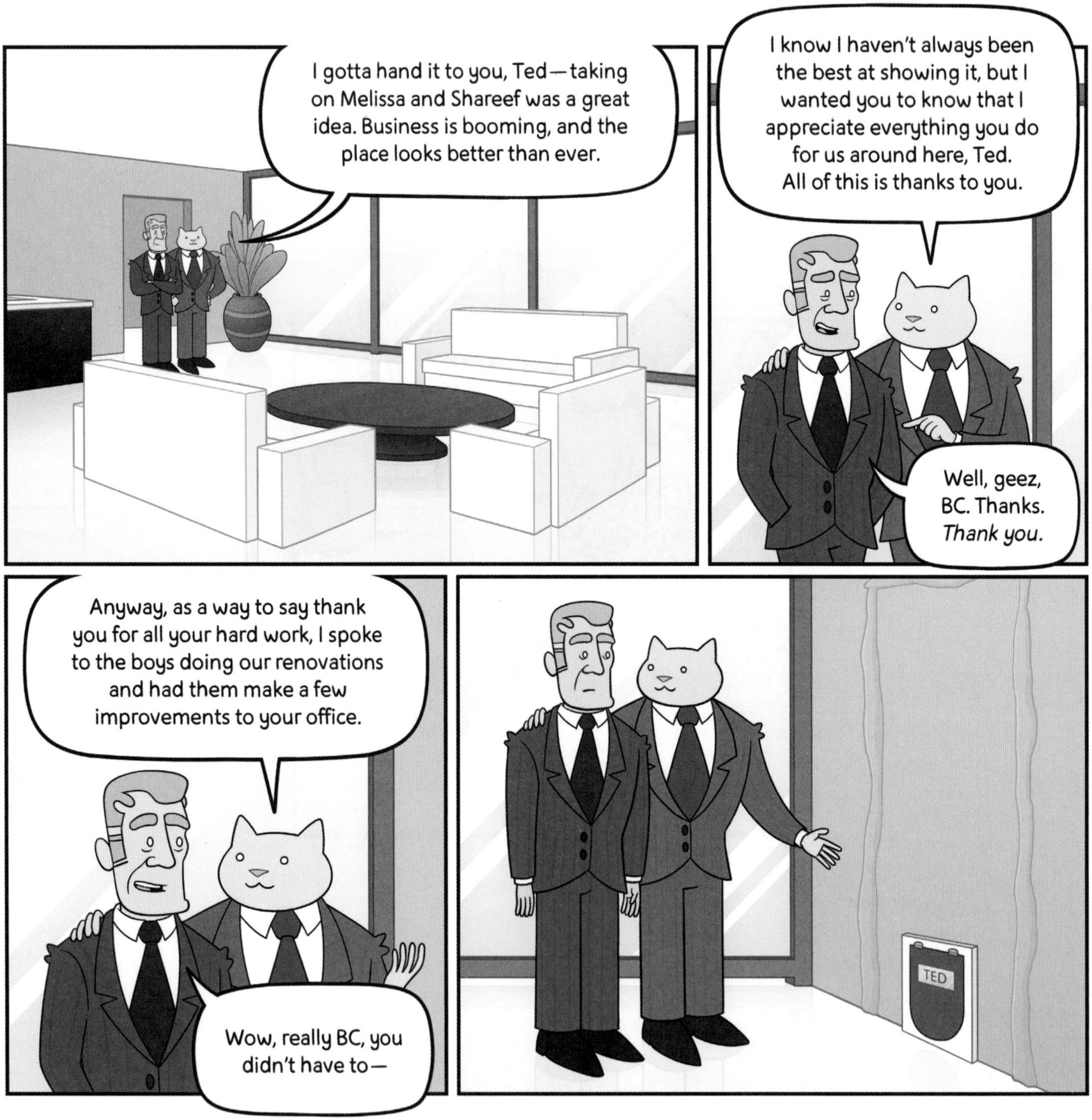

I gotta hand it to you, Ted—taking on Melissa and Shareef was a great idea. Business is booming, and the place looks better than ever.
I know I haven't always been the best at showing it, but I wanted you to know that I appreciate everything you do for us around here, Ted. All of this is thanks to you.
Well, geez, BC. Thanks. *Thank you.*
Anyway, as a way to say thank you for all your hard work, I spoke to the boys doing our renovations and had them make a few improvements to your office.
Wow, really BC, you didn't have to—
TED

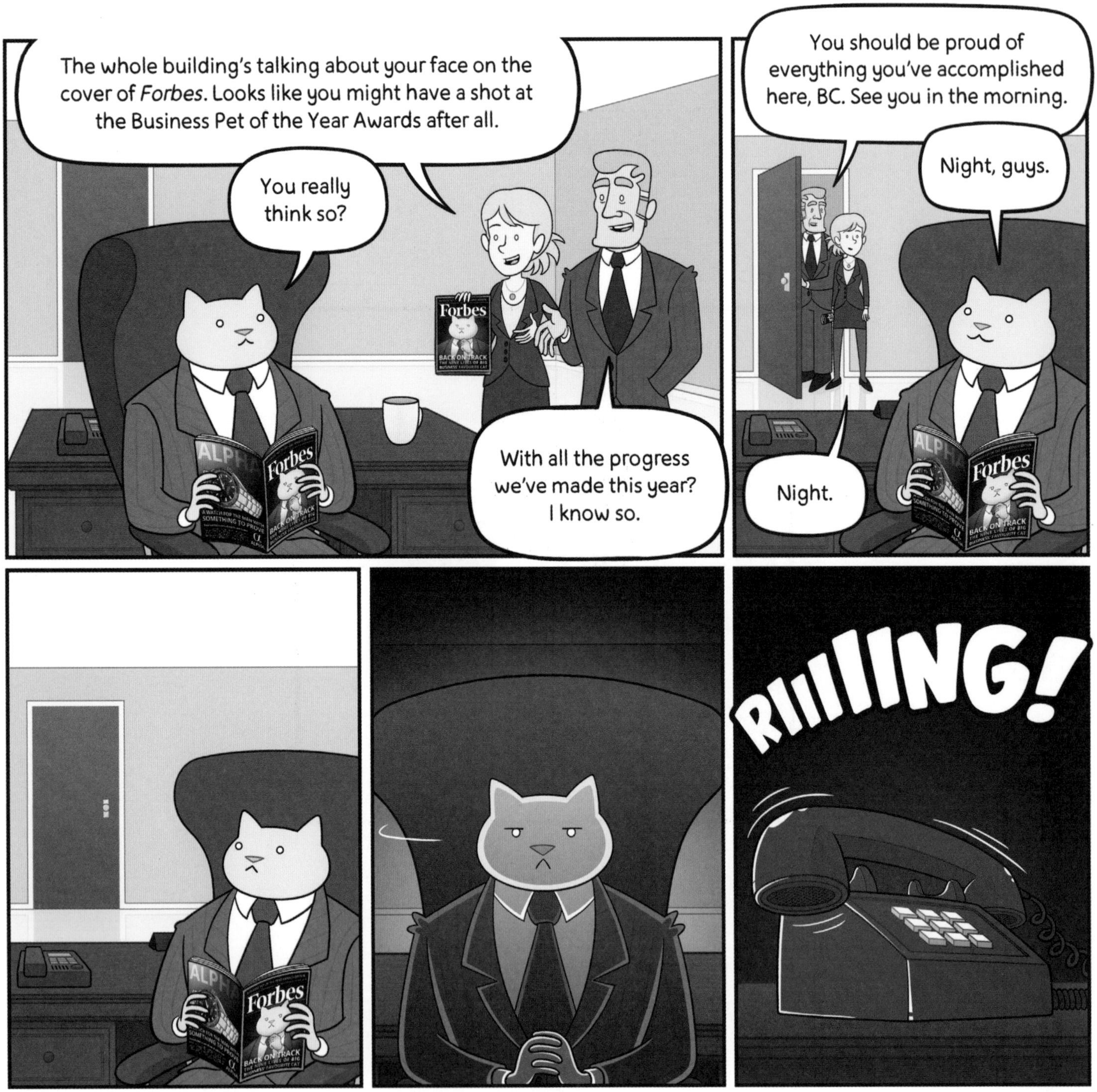
The whole building's talking about your face on the cover of *Forbes*. Looks like you might have a shot at the Business Pet of the Year Awards after all.
You really think so?
With all the progress we've made this year? I know so.
Forbes
BACK ON TRACK
You should be proud of everything you've accomplished here, BC. See you in the morning.
Night, guys.
Night.
RIIIIING!

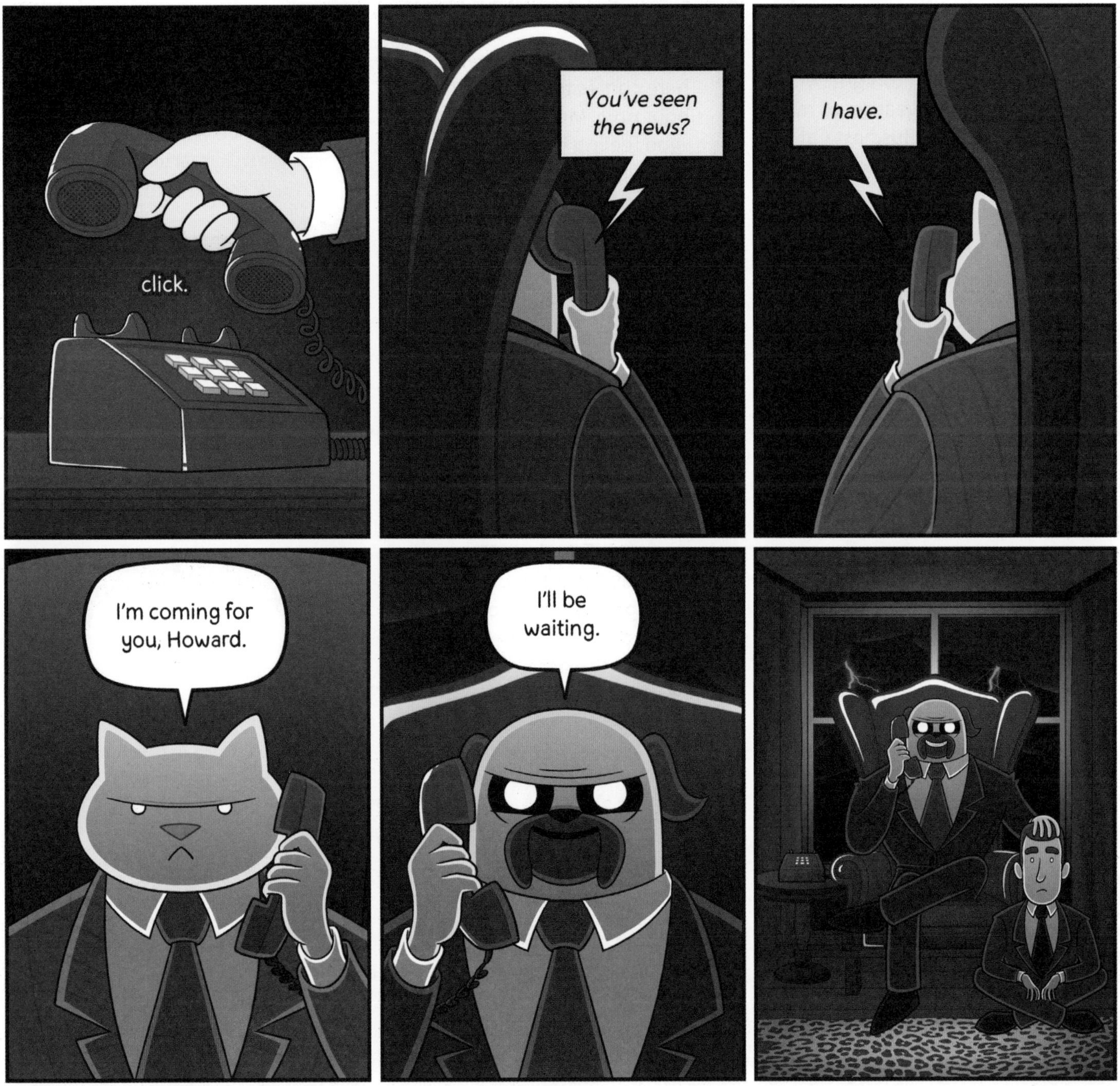
click.
You've seen the news?
I have.
I'm coming for you, Howard.
I'll be waiting.

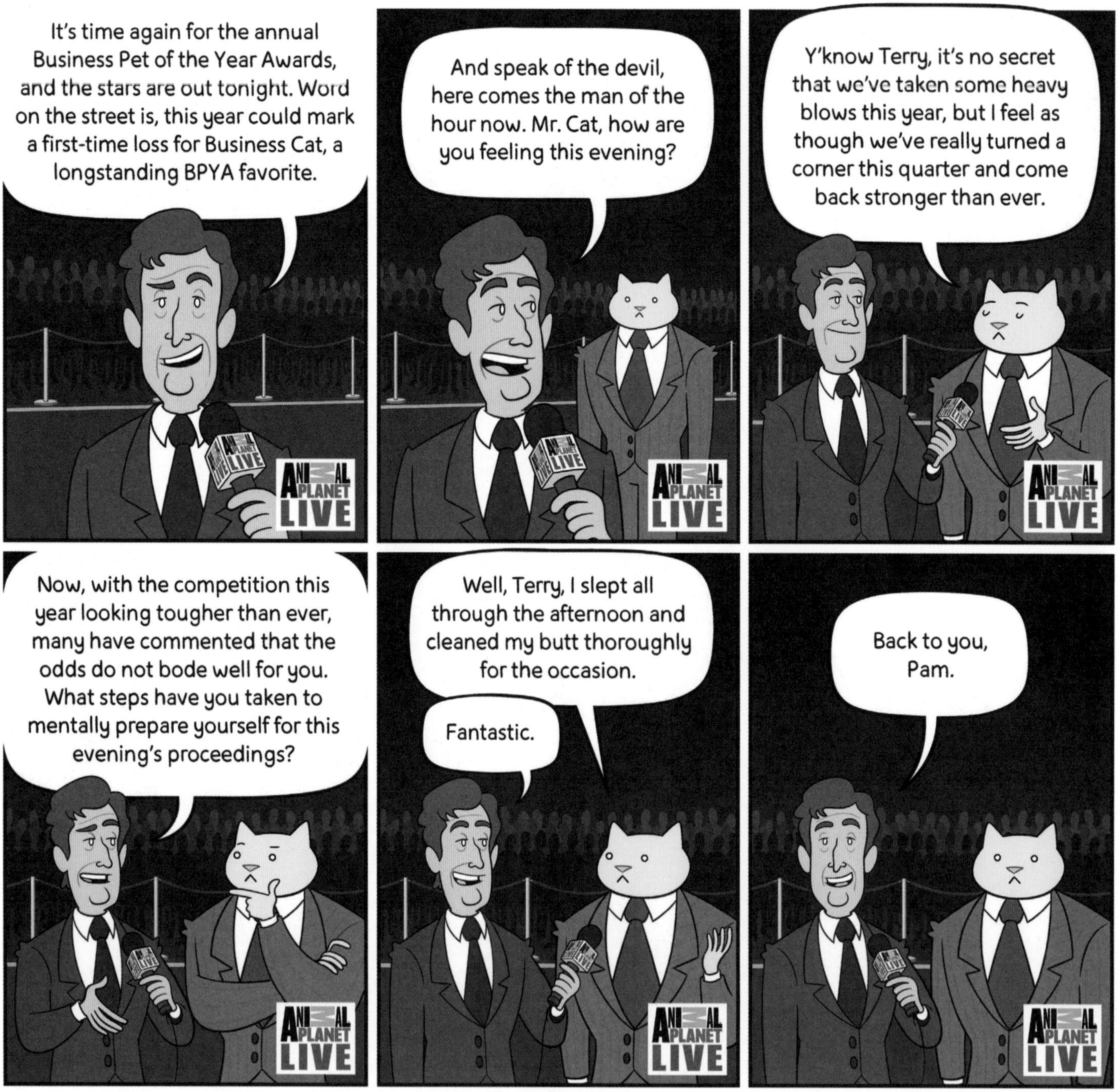
It's time again for the annual Business Pet of the Year Awards, and the stars are out tonight. Word on the street is, this year could mark a first-time loss for Business Cat, a longstanding BPYA favorite.
And speak of the devil, here comes the man of the hour now. Mr. Cat, how are you feeling this evening?
Y'know Terry, it's no secret that we've taken some heavy blows this year, but I feel as though we've really turned a corner this quarter and come back stronger than ever.
Now, with the competition this year looking tougher than ever, many have commented that the odds do not bode well for you. What steps have you taken to mentally prepare yourself for this evening's proceedings?
Well, Terry, I slept all through the afternoon and cleaned my butt thoroughly for the occasion.
Fantastic.
Back to you, Pam.

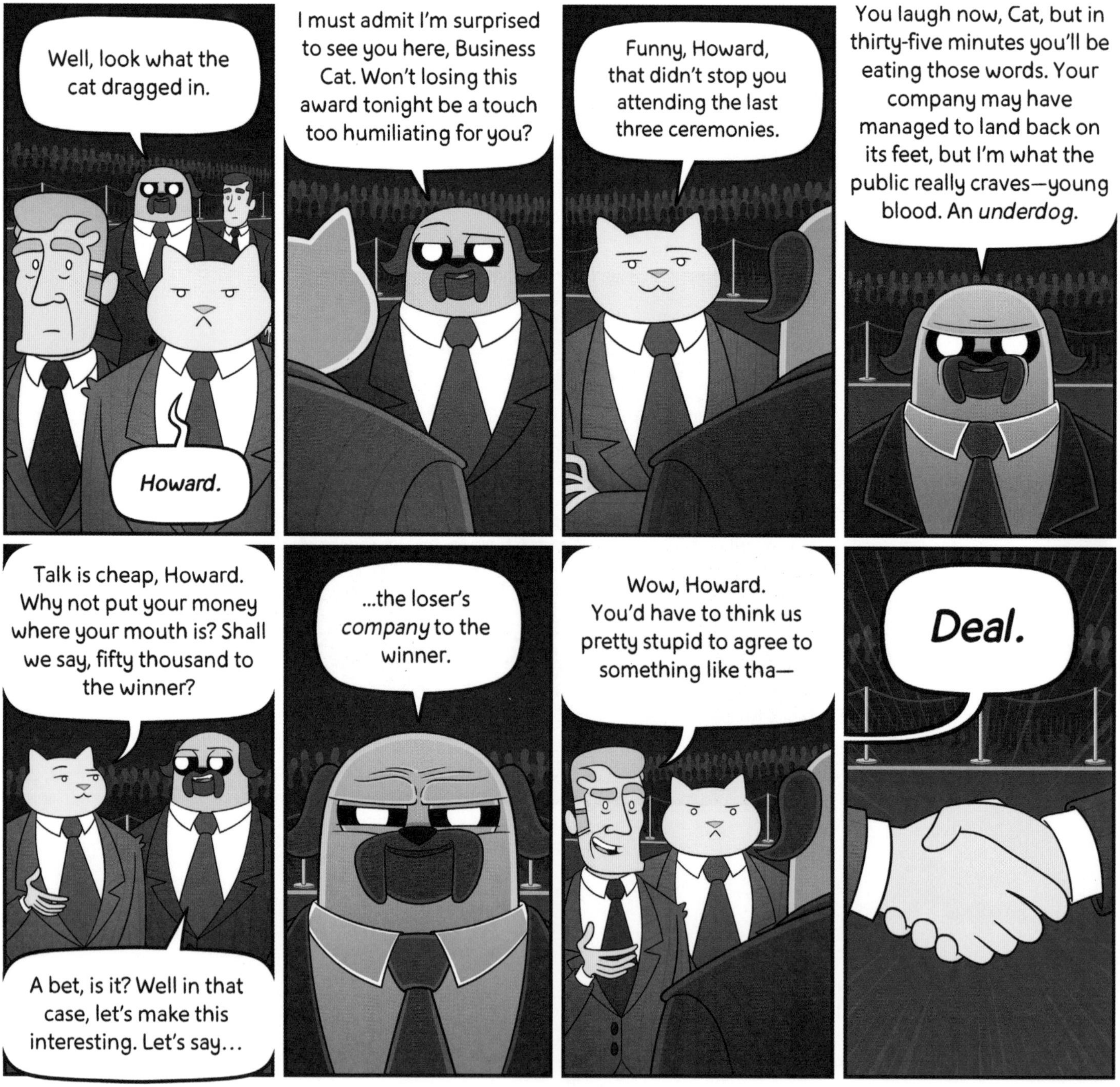
Well, look what the cat dragged in.
Howard.
I must admit I'm surprised to see you here, Business Cat. Won't losing this award tonight be a touch too humiliating for you?
Funny, Howard, that didn't stop you attending the last three ceremonies.
You laugh now, Cat, but in thirty-five minutes you'll be eating those words. Your company may have managed to land back on its feet, but I'm what the public really craves—young blood. An *underdog*.
Talk is cheap, Howard. Why not put your money where your mouth is? Shall we say, fifty thousand to the winner?
A bet, is it? Well in that case, let's make this interesting. Let's say…
...the loser's *company* to the winner.
Wow, Howard. You'd have to think us pretty stupid to agree to something like tha—
Deal.

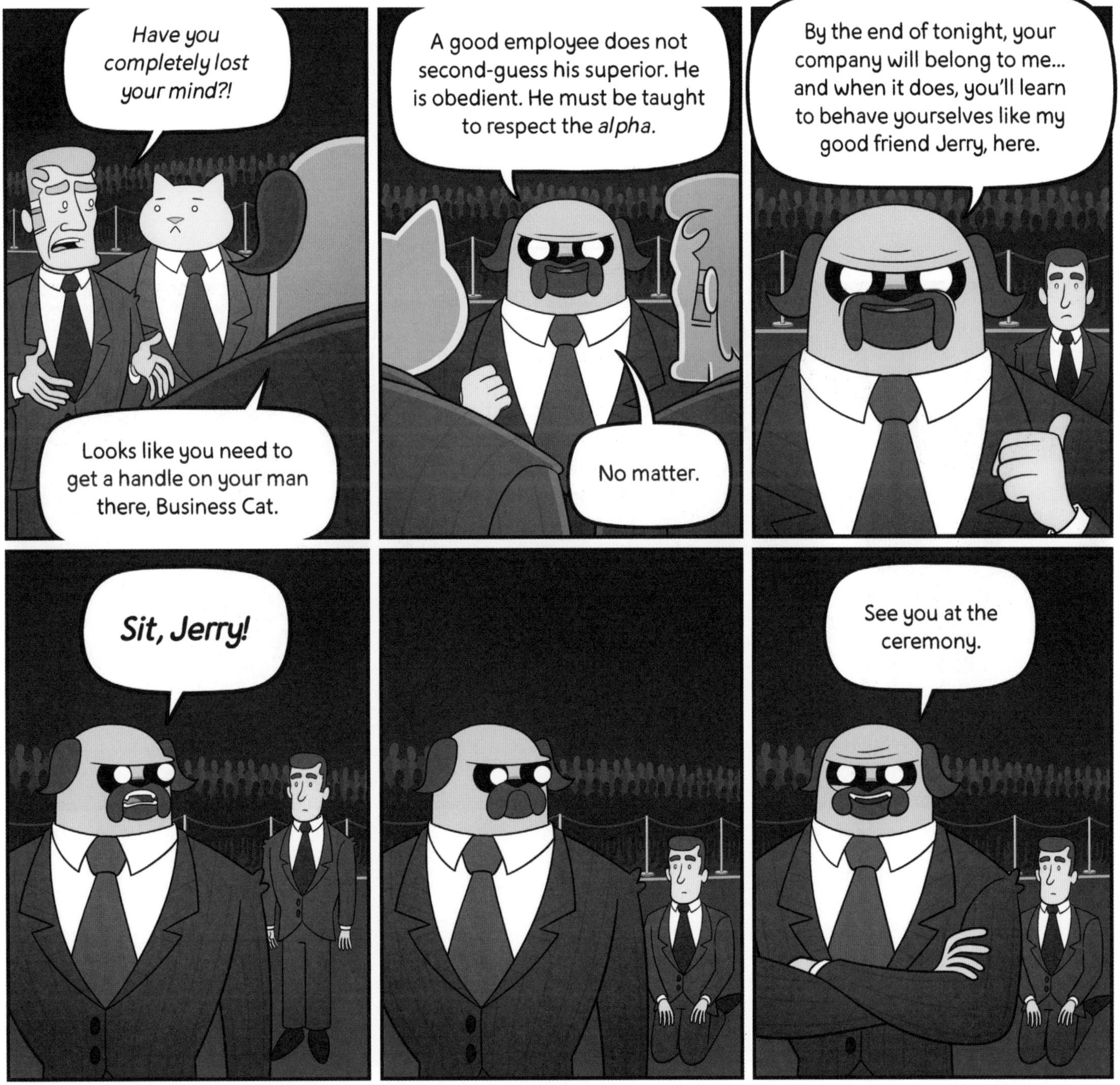
Have you completely lost your mind?!
Looks like you need to get a handle on your man there, Business Cat.
A good employee does not second-guess his superior. He is obedient. He must be taught to respect the *alpha*.
No matter.
By the end of tonight, your company will belong to me... and when it does, you'll learn to behave yourselves like my good friend Jerry, here.
Sit, Jerry!
See you at the ceremony.

I hope you know what you're doing, Cat.
So do I.
Ladies and gentlemen, welcome to the fifth annual Business Pet of the Year Awards. Before we begin with tonight's proceedings, we'd like to take this time to remember the titans of industry we lost this year. Truly, they will be missed.
BUSINESS PET OF THE YEAR AWARDS
IN MEMORIAM
PICKLES
2002 - 2015
P
FISH
JAN - FEB

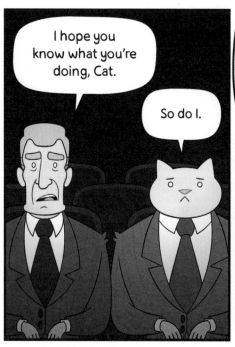

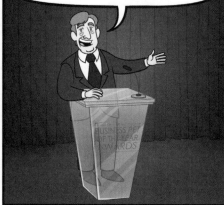

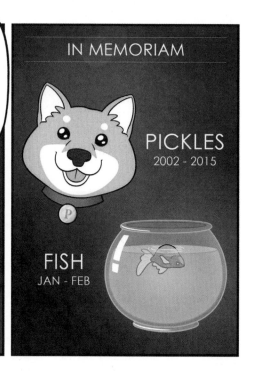

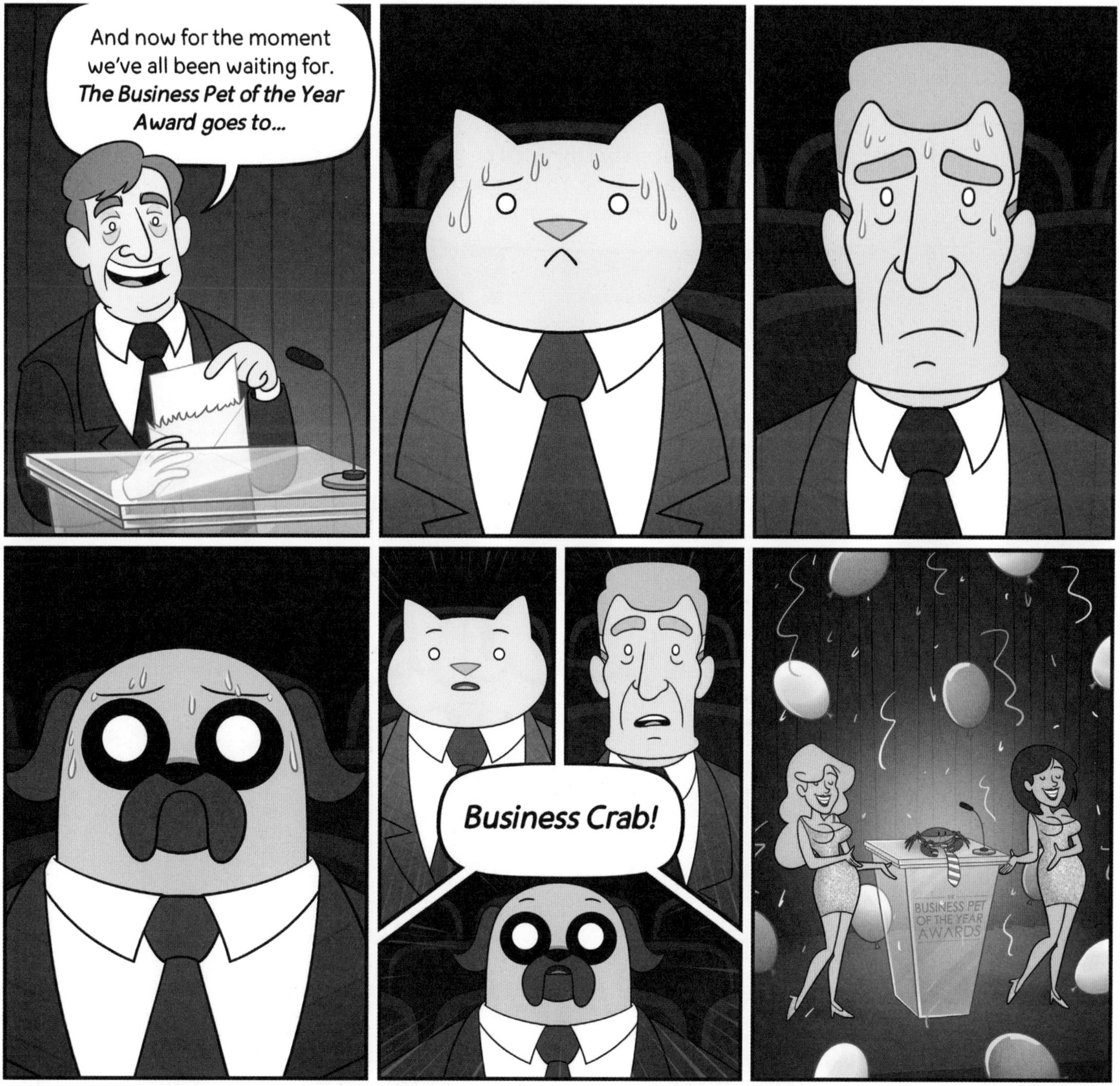
And now for the moment we've all been waiting for. *The Business Pet of the Year Award goes to...*
Business Crab!
BUSINESS PET OF THE YEAR AWARDS

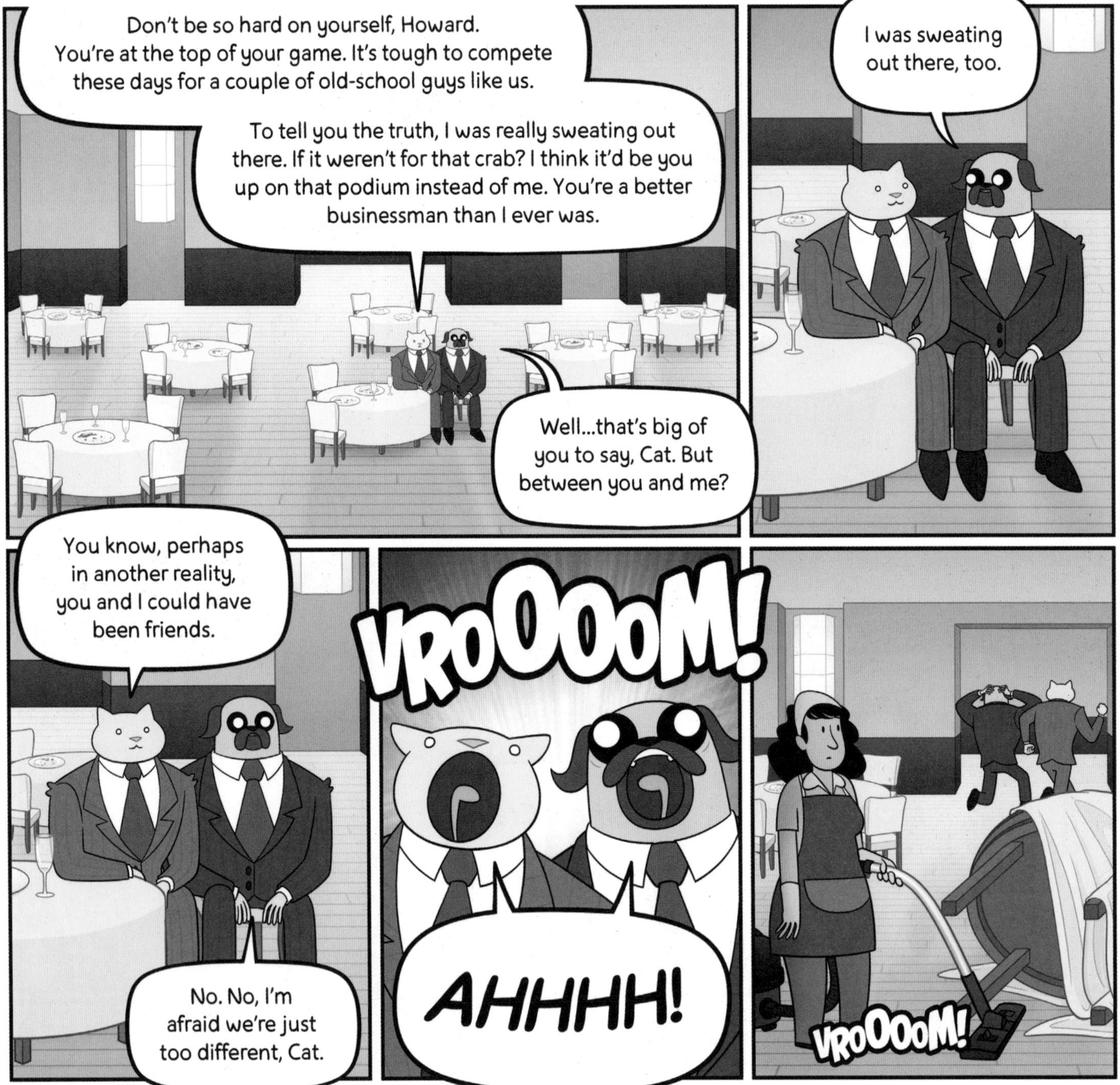
Don't be so hard on yourself, Howard. You're at the top of your game. It's tough to compete these days for a couple of old-school guys like us.
To tell you the truth, I was really sweating out there. If it weren't for that crab? I think it'd be you up on that podium instead of me. You're a better businessman than I ever was.
Well...that's big of you to say, Cat. But between you and me?
I was sweating out there, too.
You know, perhaps in another reality, you and I could have been friends.
No. No, I'm afraid we're just too different, Cat.
VROOOOOM!
AHHHH!
VROOOOM!

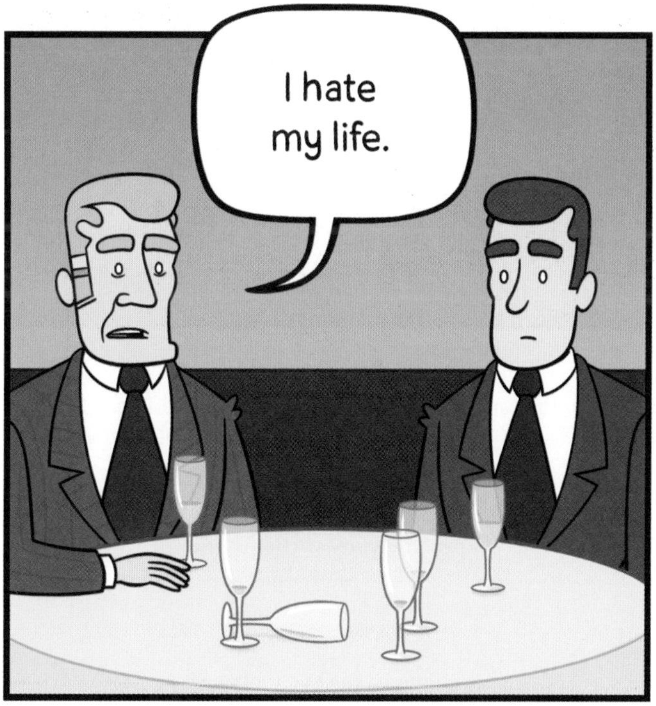
I hate my life.

BUSINESS CAT

Andrews McMeel Publishing
a division of Andrews McMeel Universal
1130 Walnut Street, Kansas City, Missouri 64106

www.andrewsmcmeel.com

16 17 18 19 20 SDB 10 9 8 7 6 5 4 3 2 1

ISBN: 978-1-4494-7414-0

Library of Congress Control Number: 2016937753

Editor: Grace Suh
Art Director: Holly Ogden
Production Manager: Chuck Harper
Production Editor: Erika Kuster

Attention: Schools and Businesses